Popular Rhymes and Sayings of Ireland

Popular Rhymes

and

Sayings of Ireland

JOHN J. MARSHALL

Third Edition

BOOKS ULSTER

Second edition, rewritten and enlarged, published in 1931 by the author and printed in Dungannon by the Tyrone Printing Company, Limited.

This new, third edition published in 2015.

Typographical arrangement, design, layout © Books Ulster

ISBN: 978-1-910375-03-7

The front cover illustration accompanies the poem "Peg of Limavady" in the 1902 edition of W. M. Thackeray's *The Irish Sketch Book*.

FOREWORD

John Johnson Marshall (1862-1944) was born and grew up near the Dyan in County Tyrone. He was a draper by trade and spent the greater part of his working life in the employment of the Robinson and Cleaver department store in Donegall Square, Belfast. He was also an amateur historian and folklorist who published a number of books and pamphlets on local history and culture, mostly in his latter years. The majority of these publications have become extremely scarce and practically unobtainable today. Among them are *History of Charlemont Fort and Borough*, *History of Dungannon*, *Clochar na Righ*, *The Romance of Dundonald*, *Old Belfast* and *Irish Tories, Rapparees and Robbers*.

Popular Rhymes and Sayings of Ireland was first issued in 1924 as a forty-two page pamphlet, but Marshall greatly revised and enlarged the work for a 1931 second edition in which he added numerous riddles, tongue-twisters, charms and further rhymes, while removing a chapter on 'The Irish Rivers mentioned in Edmund Spenser's Poems'. This new, third edition, is a reprint of the expanded second edition, but with endnotes added to explain some vocabulary and to provide additional background information. A number of spelling, punctuation and typographical errors in the original have been corrected, although undoubtedly others will have been overlooked and perhaps a few more created. However, it is hoped that the changes have generally been for the good. The endnotes are by the editor, the footnotes by Marshall.

A debt of gratitude is owed to John J. Marshall for preserving in print what might otherwise have been lost, for although he reproduced material that can be found in other sources he also recorded rhymes, riddles and other traditions which probably cannot. Many of the latter he recalled from his own childhood or was informed of by friends. He had the intelligence, foresight and cultural awareness to appreciate their worth when others didn't, as he remarks in Chapter XXVI:

"The foregoing (riddle) was picked up by the writer when a boy in his native county Tyrone, amongst much other material classed as rubbish by his wiser seniors."

This book is not only an informative and entertaining read for the layman enthusiast, but an invaluable addition to the collection of any social historian interested in Ireland.

Derek Rowlinson

Bangor,

January 2015

CONTENTS

CHAP.   PAGE

    I. Nursery rhymes; children's rhymes.   1

   II. Children's play rhymes; their different versions.   10

  III. Further play rhymes and singing games; their
        different versions.   20

  IV. Further singing games; their different versions.   28

   V. Children's school games and rhymes; tongue
        twisters; schoolboy spelling; Xmas games.   35

  VI. Children's school games and rhymes; tongue
        twisters; schoolboy spelling; Xmas games.   40

 VII. Christmas Rhymers.   46

VIII. Two Tyrone versions of Christmas Rhyme.   53

  IX. The wren boys; the wren song; remote antiquity
        of the custom.   63

   X. Rhymes, complimentary, humorous and sarcastic,
        of the counties of Derry and Antrim.   75

  XI. Armagh rhymes, topographical and tory hunting.   86

 XII. Tyrone and Fermanagh Rhymes.   92

XIII. Sweet County Down: its rhymes and sayings.   98

XIV. Rhymes of the counties of Monaghan, Cavan,
        Leitrim and Westmeath.   104

 XV. Galway, Kildare, and Dublin rhymes and sayings.   111

XVI. Rhymes and sayings of the counties of Wicklow,
        Wexford and Tipperary.   119

XVII. Kilkenny rhymes and sayings; the Kilkenny cats.   125

XVIII.	County Limerick rhymes and sayings; Garryowen; on the nail.	132
XIX.	Cork; rhymes of the beautiful city and county; pleasant Bandon; Blarney.	137
XX.	Rhymes and sayings of the kingdom of Kerry.	144
XXI.	Food and boxty rhymes.	149
XXII.	Weather rhymes and sayings; moon rhymes.	154
XXIII.	Medical charms; lovers' charms; advice to bachelors; plant lore.	161
XXIV.	General Sayings.	167
XXV.	General Sayings continued.	174
XXVI.	Riddles.	178
XXVII.	Riddles continued.	188
XXVIII.	War cries of the Irish septs and Anglo-Irish barons.	196
XXIX.	Names for the northern and southern halves of Ireland; characteristics of the four provinces.	204
XXX.	Names under which Ireland was personified in the seventeenth century; the Emerald Isle.	210
XXXI.	Earliest names of Ireland; Milesian names for the island; the Isle of Saints.	215
NOTES		219

CHAPTER I.

Nursery rhymes; children's rhymes.

Rhymes and sayings form an integral part of our everyday speech and conversation from the cradle to the grave. If grown-ups have their rhymes and sayings much more so have children. The youthful imagination can conjure up scenes and happenings in the magic land of Make-Believe, within whose enchanted portals those who have attained to maturity may not pass.

Who were the authors of these rhymes? Were they composed by children more gifted than their fellows, or were there nameless Lewis Carrolls who preferred to remain unknown to fame and to be satisfied with the reward of having afforded a new pleasure to the little ones. We ask, but the question remains unanswered, and we are never likely to know the names of laureates of the nursery and playground.

"Have you ever been to Ireland, reader? Have you ever walked her four roads and the plains of Meath? Have you ever struggled along the rocky road to Dublin:—

> "Jip, jip, my little horse,
> Jip, jip, again, sir;
> How many miles to Dublin Town?
> Three score and ten, sir."

In such pleasant fashion with a verse of a nursery rhyme does Sir William Orpen, R.A., the famous painter, begin his delightful book, "Stories of old Ireland and Myself."

There is a story in an old Irish magazine of 1817 where amongst the incidents narrated it says:—"To no purpose did the perplexed Irish soldier dandle the babe in his arms, singing:—

> "Here we go uppy, up uppy,
> And here we go downy, down downy,
> And now we go this and that way,
> And high for Dublin towny!"

The nurse to amuse a fractious child will cry:—

> "Cuckoo, cherry tree,
> Catch a wee bird and give it to me."

In England as well as in Germany, it is a belief amongst the peasantry that the cuckoo, if asked, will tell you by the repetition of her cry, how many years you have to live. Hence the rhyme:—

> "Cuckoo, cherry tree,
> Good bird tell me
> How many years I have to live."

Kelly, in his "Indo-European Tradition and Folklore," ascribes the allusion to the cherry tree in this and similar rhymes, to the superstition that before the cuckoo ceases her song she must eat three good meals of cherries. (Dyer: "English Folk-Lore, I. 58-9, 2nd ed.)

Another rhyme used to interest a restless child is:—

> "I have a wee puppet I keep in my pocket,
>   I feed it on corn and hay—
> There came a wee man and he swore by his sowl
>   He would steal my wee puppet away—
>   Nor you, nor you, nor you,"

pointing to the members of the household about,

> "But a nice wee boy like you."

When small children are being nursed upon the knee their elders frequently dandle them up and down to the words:—

> "This is the way the ladies ride,
>   Gently pacing, gently pacing—

suiting the action to the words, then after a little,

> "This is the way the gentlemen ride,
>   Gallop and trot, gallop and trot—

with quickened motion to suit.

This is all the length that the performance goes in the North of Ireland, but in Scotland they have an additional couplet—

> "This is the way the cadgers ride,
>   Creels and a'! creels and a'!! creels and a'!!!

by which time the equestrian action has become violent.

In no long time after the horseback ride perhaps Johnnie Nod puts in an appearance, and it is then:

> "To bed, to bed," says Sleepy Head,
>   "Time enough," says Slow;
> "Put on the pot," says Greedy Guts,
>   "We'll eat before we go."

Slightly varied this rhyme is to be found in both England and Scotland, as are a great many of the rhymes given in this series.

Here is a rhyme repeated by nurse or mother as she puts the tiny shoe or slipper on some little toddler's chubby foot:—

> "Jack Smith, of Monterlony,
> Can you shoe this pony?
> Yes indeed, and that I can
> As well as any other man.
> Rise Jack—strike Tom,
> Blow the bellows, old man,
> Here's a nail, and here's a prod,
> Gee-up, John—horsey's shod."

There is a variant of the first two lines:—

> "Jack Smith, filly fine,
> Can you shoe this horse of mine?"

Then there is the affecting story of a near relative of the 'Old Woman who lived in a Shoe':—

> "There was an old woman who lived in a lamp,
> She had no room to pound her champ,*
> So she up with her beetle[1] and broke the lamp,
> And then she had room to pound her champ!"

---

* Mashing potatoes. [N.B. Champ is an Ulster dish of mashed potatoes mixed with chopped scallions (spring onions)].

Another nursery rhyme owes its origin to the disbanded soldiers and younger sons of gentlemen who had lost their means of living after the rebellion of 1641. Many of these men took to the woods and maintained themselves by the spoil of law-abiding subjects, hence they were called *Tories*.

> "Ho, brother Teig, what is your story?
> I went to the wood and shot a Tory;
> I went to the wood and shot another,
> Was it the same, or was it his brother?
> I hunted him in, I hunted him out,
> Three times through the bog, out and about,
> Till out through the bush I spied his head,
> So I levelled my gun and shot him dead."

The following is an English nursery version of the Irish rhyme:—

> "I'll tell you a story about John M'Rory,
> He went to the wood and shot a Tory,
> Then he went back and told his brother,
> And went to the wood and shot another."

This is quite lacking in the dramatic action of the original rhyme.

An account of Tories and Tory hunting will be found in the writer's "Irish Tories, Rapparees and Robbers."

Another rhyme of the nursery class is:—

> "I went to the fair of Dungannon,
>   And bought a three-halfpenny pig—
> I carried it home in my apron,
>   And danced a swaggering jig."

What could be more affecting than this county Tyrone rhyme:—

> "My uncle Tom's an honest man,
>   And that of good profession,
> He'd dance a jig on a pratie[2] rig
>   When men and dogs were sleeping,"

and the following breathes the essence of hospitality:—

> "My aunt Jane she took me in,
> And gave me tea in her wee tin;
> A big round bap[3] with sugar on the top,
> And three black lumps[4] from her wee shop."

Another rhyme common amongst little folks, who are all unwitting of its interesting associations, is:—

> "When I was young and had no sense
> I bought a wee fiddle for eighteen pence,
> And all the tune that I could play
> Was 'Over the hills and far away'."

Another version of it is:—

> "Daniel donn the piper's son
> Stole and ate a penny bun;
> And all the tune that he could play
> Was 'Over the hills and far away'."

"Over the hills and far away" has been common property throughout Great Britain as a song and as a saying for at least two centuries. There is a copy of the tune in the Pepysian Collection, and it is reprinted in the appendix to Motherwell's "Minstrelsy," p. 355. It has been traced to the year 1715 as an Irish Jacobite ditty deploring the exile of James, son of the deposed monarch, James II., but it is much older than that. A song with this name was written by John M'Donnell (Claragh) who was born in 1691 and died in 1754. A version of this song was sung in the "Beggar's Opera" in 1728 as a duet for Polly and Macheath, and created a great sensation.

The rhyme was perhaps suggested by "Jockey's Lamentation" in "Wit and Mirth, or Pills to Purge Melancholy," 1709, where the words and tune of "Over the hills and far away" are to be found in the fourth volume.

> "Tom he was a piper's son,
> He learned to play when he was young,
> But all the tunes that he could play
> Was 'Over the hills and far away.'
> Over the hills and a great way off,
> And the wind will blow my top-knot off."
>
> (S. J. A. Fitz-gerald: *Stories of Famous Songs*, pp. 353-5.)

———•◆•———

The following protective charm, known as the *White Paternoster*, common in Ireland, is not only known wherever the English language is spoken, but is common throughout Europe. Miss R. N. Busk collected a number of versions of it in Italy. This is the version that the writer learned in Ulster:—

> "Matthew, Mark, Luke and John,
> Bless the bed that I lie on.
> There are four corners to my bed,
> Around them are four angels spread,
> And if I die before I wake,
> I pray the Lord my soul to take."

Douglas Hyde says ("Religious Songs of Conacht"):—"It is curious to find the same rhyme in Gaelic in Co. Mayo translated it runs:—

> "Four corners to my bed,
> Four angels round it spread;
> If I die before the morning,
> In heaven may my soul be dawning."

Or again in Aran, where it is closer to the English form;—

> "Four posts round my bed,
> Four angels have it spread;
> Matthew, Mark, Luke and John;
> Keep me O God till the day shall dawn."

As the children grow older their advance in years is still accompanied by suitable rhymes such as:—

> "Indeed and doubles,
> Spades and shovels,
> Curly kale and pratie stalks."

A snail rhyme in the south of Ireland repeated by children when they see that common mollusc is:—

> "Shell a muddy, shell a muddy,
>   Put out your horns,
>   For the king's daughter is coming to town
>   With a red petticoat and a green gown."

In the north of Ireland when the children see a hairy caterpillar they address it as:—

> "Grannie greybeard, without tooth or tongue,
>   Give me your wee finger and I'll give you my thumb."

Jack Spratt and his good wife are well known to English children, but Ireland has her own localised form of the legend in which a much more affecting state of affairs is disclosed than is to be found in the Saxon description of the appetites of Mr. Spratt and his spouse. Here is the calamitous effect produced by the balanced appetites of this interesting couple:—

> "Jack Spratt could eat no fat,
>   And his wife could eat no lean;
> So between them both
>   Poor Paddy was left behind."

The pair left the platter as bare as Mother Hubbard's cupboard. Another Irish version of a well-known English rhyme is:—

> "The lion and the unicorn
>   Fighting for the crown,
> Up jumps a wee dog
>   And knocks them both down."

A further English rhyme that used to be common in the North of Ireland was:—

> "Up and down the City Road,
>   In and out the Eagle;
> That's the way the money goes,
>   Pop goes the weasel.
> "A halfpenny for a cotton ball,
>   A farthing for a needle;
> That's the way money goes,
>   Pop goes the weasel."

This was originally a portion of a comic song in a burlesque performance at the Haymarket Theatre, London, in the year 1855, and although the song itself has been forgotten, the above few lines of it have been adopted as a nursery rhyme, and have still a certain amount of currency.

Here are two further rhymes:—

> "Crow, crow, your nest's afire, and all your young ones dead—
> A wee pot of porridge before you go to bed."

While the small girls sing:—

> "I have a bonnet trimmed with blue,
> Why don't you wear it? So I do.
> When I go to meet my John,
> Then I put my bonnet on."

Here is a little rhyme that small children used to repeat to misses in their teens as well as to more mature young ladies:—

> "If you be a fair maid, as I suppose you be,
> You'll neither laugh nor smile at the tickling of your knee,"

accompanying the action to the word.

Time passes on with child as well as with the adult, and the little ones who had the foregoing rhymes said or sung to them are now beginning to have rhymes and games on their own account.

A very interesting little rhyme and game of this class is described by Patrick Kennedy in his charming old-fashioned book, "Evenings in the Duffrey," (p. 63).

Shaving the White Friar.

"The children are ensconced in the laps or between the legs of seniors, except three who are performing the ticklish operation of 'Shaving the White Friar.' Having reared a small cone of turf ashes they stick a straw upright in its summit, and each in turn scrapes away a portion of the heap, repeating at each operation:—

> "Shave the White Friar,
> Draw a little nigher;
> If the Friar chance to fall,
> Your back will pay for all."

When the straw falls, which it must do sooner or later, the last operator must suffer in body or goods; a general cuffing being the usual reward for his awkwardness."

The foregoing game as described by Kennedy was played in county Wexford one hundred years ago, and may be played there still. The writer knows of it being played in county Armagh sixty or seventy years ago under the name of "Shave the bold Friar."

Another childish game is

Carry My Lady to London.

In playing this two children grasp each other by the wrists, forming a seat, on which another child sits, who is thus carried about, while the bearers sing:—

> "Give me a pin to stick in my shin,
> To carry my lady to London;
> Give me another to stick in my other,
> To carry her a little bit further."

In Ireland this is merely a child's rhyme without any significance attaching to it, but in some parts of England—Derbyshire and Worcestershire, for instance—pin shows are, or were, at any rate, common twenty-five or thirty years ago, where the exhibitions consisted principally of daisies and buttercups, with occasionally where procurable, a large and bright flower in the centre, all pressed between two pieces of glass and carried around wrapped in brown paper. The rhyme repeated was "Give me a pin to stick in my chin." Upon payment of the pin, the picture was uncovered and exhibited to the payee. In some districts this game, or rather proceeding, was called "Pinaseed," which was merely the shortened or slurred form of the formula, "a pin to see it."

CHAPTER II.

Children's play rhymes; their different versions.

Of great interest to the Folk-lorist are the numerous rhymes sung by children at their games, many of which have come down from time immemorial, and whose origins are lost in the mists of antiquity. The little stanza given by Sir William Orpen, as quoted at the beginning of Chapter I. is a nursery adaptation of the first verse of a singing rhyme, "How many miles to Babylon?" of which some nineteen versions are given in Lady Gomme's "Traditional Games."

The following is a County Louth version:—

> "How many miles to Babylon?
>   Three score and ten.
> Can I get there by candle-light?
>   There and back again.
> Here's my black (raising one foot),
> And here's my blue (raising the other),
> Open the gates and let me through."

Here is the Belfast version:—

> "How many miles to Barney Bridge?
>   Threescore and ten.
> Will I be there by candle-light?
>   Yes, if your legs are long.
> If you please will you let the kind's horses through
>   Yes, but take care of the hindmost one."

This is how they play it in Dublin:—

> "How many miles to Barney Bridge?
>   Threescore and ten.
> Will I be there by Candlemas?
>   Yes, and back again.

———— ♦ ————

A courtesy to you, another to you,
And pray fair maids, will you let us through?
Thro' and thro' you shall go for the king's sake,
But take care the last man does not meet a mistake."

Another rhyme of which there is a Scottish form of words which differ considerably from the Irish version, being also sung to a different tune, is:—

Here's an Oul' Widow.

This is a mixed boys and girls' game, and is played as follows:— All join hands to form a ring. A girl takes her stand in the centre, the rest walking or dancing round and singing:—

"Oh, here's an oul' widow, she lies alone
Oh, here's an oul' widow, she lies alone,
She wants a man, and she can't get none.
    Choose one, choose two,
    Choose the fairest of you;
The fairest one that I can see
Is Johnny Jones, come over to me."

Being thus favoured, Johnny leaves the ring and joins the "oul' widow." The rest then resume their dance round and sing:—

"An' now she's married an' tied till a bag,
    An' tied till a bag, an' tied till a bag,
An' now she's married an' tied till a bag,
    An' married till a man with a wooden leg."

The following is another Belfast variation:—

"There was an old soldier, he came from the wars,
    His age it was sixty and one;
Go you old soldier and choose a wife,
    Choose a good one or choose none.

Here's a poor widow, she lives her lone,
    She hasn't a daughter to marry but one;
Choose to the east, choose to the west,
    And choose to the very one you like best.

> Here's a couple married in joy,
>> First a girl and then a boy;
> Seven years after and seven years to come,
>> Pray, young couple, kiss and have done."

This seems to be a compound of the "Oul' Widow" and another play rhyme.

The Old Soldier.

> "I am an old soldier, I come from the war,
>> Come from the war,
> I am an old soldier, I come from the war,
>> And my age it is sixty and three.
>
> I have but one son and he lies alone,
>> And he lies alone.
> I have but one son and he lies alone,
>> And he's still making moan for lying alone."

A very much more characteristic form of the foregoing rhyme is to be found in the county Louth, where it was noted by Miss R. Stephens.

Here's a Soldier.

> "Here's a soldier left his lone,
> Wants a wife and can't get none.
> Merrily go round and choose your own,
> Choose a good one or choose none;
> Choose the worst or choose the best,
> Or choose the very one you like best.
>
> What's your will, my dilcy dulcy officer?
>> What's your will, my dilcy dulcy dee?
> My will is to marry, my dilcy dulcy officer,
>> My will is to marry, my dilcy, dulcy dee.
>
> Come, marry one of us, my dilcy dulcy officer
>> Come, marry one of us, my dilcy, dulcy dee;

> You're all too old and ugly, my dilcy dulcy officer
>   You're all too old and ugly, my dilcy dulcy dee.

> Thrice too good for you, sir, my dilcy dulcy officer,
> Thrice too good for you, sir, my dilcy dulcy dee.

> This couple got married, we wish them joy,
>   Every year a girl or a boy;
> And if that does not do, a hundred and two,
>   We hope the couple will kiss together."

The game is played by one child standing in the middle, while the others form a ring and dance round singing. The one in the middle chooses another before the four last lines are sung. Then the rest dance round singing these lines and kiss each other. (Evidently these lines comprised two games that have got mixed.)

William Carleton in "Larry M'Farland's Wake" ("Traits and Stories") describes a very similar game played in county Tyrone.

"It's played in this way: A ring of boys and girls is made on the flure—boy and girl about—holding one another by the hands: well and good—a young fellow gets into the middle of the ring, as 'the silly ould man.' There he stands looking at all the girls to choose a wife and in the mane time, the youngsters in the ring sing out:—

> Here's a silly ould man that lies all alone,
>   That lies all alone,
>   That lies all alone,
> Here's a silly ould man that lies all alone,
> He wants a wife and he can get none.

"When the boys and girls sing this, the 'silly ould man' must choose a wife from some of the colleens belonging to the ring. Having made choice of her, she goes into the ring along with him, and they all sing out:—

> Now, young couple, you're married together,
>   You're married together,
>   You're married together,
> You must obey your father and mother,
> And love one another like sister and brother,
> I pray, young couple, you'll kiss together!

And you may be sure this part of the marriage is not missed anyway."

"I doubt," said Andy Morrow, "that good can't come of so much kissing, marrying and coorting."

There was another singing game played at the same wake, and according to the narrator, "the next play is in the military line. You see, Mr. Morrow, the man that leads the sports, places them all on their sates, and gets from some of the girls a white handkerchief, which he ties around his hat as you would a piece of mourning; he then walks round two or three times singing:

> Will you list and come with me, fair maid?
> Will you list and come with me, fair maid?
> Will you list and come with me, fair maid?
> And follow the lad with the white cockade?

When he sings this he takes off his hat and puts it on the girl he likes best, who rises and puts her arm round him, and then they both go about in the same way singing the same words. She then puts the hat on some young man, who gets up and goes round with them, singing as before. He next puts it on the girl he loves best, who, after singing and going round in the same manner, puts it on another, and he on his sweetheart and so on. This is called the **White Cockade**. When it is all over, that is, when every young man has pitched upon the girl he wishes to be his sweetheart, they sit down and sing songs and coort as they did at the marrying."

Cases of singing rhymes getting mixed are, as already shown, not at all uncommon. The following example from Holywood, county Down, collected by Miss C. M. Patterson, is made up of two different sets of words:

Pretty Little Girl of Mine.

> "See what a pretty little girl I am,
> She gave me a bottle of wine:
> Many a bottle of wine and biscuit, too,
> See what a pretty little girl can do.

On the carpet you shall kneel.
Stand up straight all in the field,
Choose the one you love best.

Now we are married and hope we enjoy,
First a girl and then a boy;
Seven years after and seven years to come,
You, young couple, kiss and have done."

A south Devonshire version of the foregoing, collected by Miss
R. H. Busk, which may be quoted for comparison, is as follows:—

See What a Pretty Little Girl Can do.

"See what a pretty little girl have I,
She brings me many a bottle of wi',
A bottle of wine and biscuits too,
See what a little girl can do.

On the carpet she shall kneel,
As the grass grows in the fiel';
Stand up straight upon your feet,
And choose the one you love so sweet."

When the couple enter the ring the tag is:—

"Now you're married we wish you joy,
First a girl and then a boy;
Seven years after son and daughter,
May you couple kiss together."

The last verse as given in "Shropshire Folk-lore" p. 509, is the best
of the variants:—

"Now you're married, I wish you joy,
First a girl and then a boy;
Seven years now and seven years to come,
Take her, kiss her, and send her home."

Very popular is the singing game with the quaint title of

Green Gravel.

"Green gravel, green gravel, your grass is so green,
The fairest young damsel that ever was seen;
I washed her in milk and rolled her in silk,
And wrote down her name with a glass pen and ink.
Dear Annie, your true love is dead—
I send you a letter to turn round your head."

The players take hands singing and walking round in a ring. The girl named turns her head and walks the reverse way, then joins the ring; this is continued till all the players are gone over.

There is a Scots or English game called "Growing Apples," in which four lines of the above rhyme occur, commencing with "We'll wash you in milk, etc."

The following form of the rhyme was noted and described by Miss Jennings, Belfast Model School, many years ago:—

"Here we're set upon green grass,
Green grass, green grass;
Here we're set upon the green grass
As green as any flower.

[Mary Murray's] stole away,
Stole away, stole away;
[Mary Murray's] stole away,
Stole away, stole away.

It's well seen by her pale face,
Pale face, pale face;
It's well seen by her pale face,
She may turn her face to the wall."

Another favourite is:—

"Down on the carpet you shall kneel,
While the grass grows at your feet—
Stand up straight upon your feet,
And choose the one you love so sweet.

Now they are married, life enjoy,
First a girl and then a boy;
Seven years after and seven years to come,
Fire on the mountains, run boys, run."

The players all take hands and move round the one who kneels in the centre, then when they come to "stand up straight upon your feet" the one in the middle stands up and chooses one out of the ring and the two dance round while the others sing the second verse, after which the first players join the ring and the game goes on.

The following is a county Dublin version of the widely diffused rhyme of

Wallflowers.

"Wallflowers, wallflowers, growin' up so high,
Neither me or my baby shall ever wish to die,
Especially (girl's name), she's the prettiest flower,
She can dance and she can sing, and she can tell the hour,
With her wee-waw, wy-waw, turn her face to the wall."

In county Waterford the last line is:—

"Turn your back to the game."

Lubin.

"Here we come looby, looby,
    Here we come looby light;
Here we come looby, looby,
    All on a Saturday night.

Put your right hand in,
    Put your right hand out;
Shake it little by little
    And turn yourself about."

And so on, feet, ears, etc., ad. lib.

In the best English version (Oxford and Wakefield) the rhyme consists of fourteen four line stanzas, while the Scotch version given in Chambers' *Popular Rhymes*, pp. 137-139, is sung to the tune of "Lillebullero."

Robbers.

"Here are the robbers coining through, coming through, coming
  through,
Here are the robbers coming through, my fair lady:
What did the robbers do to you, do to you, do to you,
What did the robbers do to you, my fair lady?
Broke my watch and stole my chain, stole my chain, stole my
  chain,
Broke my watch and stole my chain, my fair lady."

Two players stand with hands held up to form an arch, through which the remainder pass in single file, usually holding on by each other, but sometimes separately. Each of the two holding hands decide on something such as a golden apple and a silver pear, or a gold piano and a silver harp—it is all one expense, so they may as well have something fine and grand. Then as the others pass through the arch the two drop their hands down on any one they choose in the line, they then, in an undertone so as not to be overheard by the others, ask the imprisoned one whether they choose the golden apple or the silver pear, and according to their choice leave the line and take their stand on either side of the arch. This goes on until all have been chosen. By this time both sides are fairly evenly balanced, and the performance ends with a tug of war.

There is another form in which the children form two lines, when the robbers ask—"How many pounds will set us free," etc.

To which the reply is—"A hundred pounds will set you free, will set you free, will set you free."

As the robbers have not got the hundred pounds, they are informed that they will have to go to prison. To which they reply— "To prison we will not go, to prison we will not go, etc.," and as the robbers sing this reply they should have attained the end of the lines, as during the parley they were safe; but having pronounced their defiance they run away. The lines then rush headlong after them, and should they catch them, put them into the pretended prison.

A droll incident in which this rhyme played a part happened at a Christian Endeavour rally in Belfast. When the collectors were solemnly marching up the aisle to deposit their plates with the offering, some ungodly youths at the back had the impish inspiration to chant "Here are the robbers coming through, coming through, coming through." The ludicrous effect was a severe strain on the gravity of the rest of the audience.

CHAPTER III.

Further play rhymes and singing games; their different versions.

In the previous chapters there have been given two versions of the popular "How many miles to Babylon." Here is a third:—

> "How many miles to Curriglass?
> Three score and ten, sir.
> Will I be there by candle-light?
> Yes, and back again, sir."

The players join hands standing in a ring and when they have sung [the] above verse, they then shout, "Thread the long needle and sew." The players then take hands right and left alternately as they pass round the circle, forming what is called in Quadrilles "The Grand Chain." The words together with the old Irish air to which it is sung are given in "One Hundred Singing Games," edited by Frank Kidson.

The following game is played in north Tyrone. The players divide into two parties which face each other. One side sings:—

> "I'll give you the bread and wine, the bread and wine, the bread and wine,
> Hissowry, O Hissowry."

(The refrain varies slightly in different localities, it may be "Mitheery, O Hithoory" or "Mitheery, an Mithorey.")

To which the others reply:—

> "You'll not give me the bread and wine, the bread and wine, the bread and wine, etc."
> "Then I will bring a policeman, a policeman, a policeman, etc."
> "I don't care for your policeman, your policeman, your policeman, etc."
> "Then I will bring the red coat, the red coat, the red coat, the red coat, etc."

"I don't care for your red coat, your red coat, your red coat, etc."

"I see you want to rise a row, to rise a row, to rise a row, etc."

The two parties face each other advancing and receding, singing verses alternately. At the last verse they mix together and have a sham fight.

Another rhyme so popular in Tyrone that no picnic would be complete without it is:—

The Farmer's in his Den.

A ring is formed of boys, girls and grown-ups, with a young man in the middle. They move round singing:—

> "The farmer's in his den, the farmer's in his den,
> Heigh ho for Derry oh, the farmer wants a wife.
>
> "The farmer wants a wife, the farmer wants a wife,
> Heigh ho for Derry oh, the farmer wants a wife."

(The young man in the middle picks out a girl and takes her into the inside of the ring.)

> "The wife wants a child, the wife wants a child,
> Heigh ho for Derry oh, the wife wants a child."

(She picks out a little girl or boy and takes him or her into the centre.)

> "The child wants a nurse, the child wants a nurse,
> Heigh ho for Derry oh, the child wants a nurse."

(The child selects a young girl.)

> "The nurse wants a dog, the nurse wants a dog,
> Heigh ho for Derry oh, the nurse wants a dog."

(The nurse selects a young man.)

> "The dog stands his lone, the dog stands his lone,
> Heigh ho for Derry oh, the dog stands his lone."

(All clear back into the ring except the young man who is left alone in the centre, when the performance is continued over again as often as desired.)

The Belfast and county Antrim version of this singing game is slightly different. It is there played as "The Farmer is in the Dell."

"The Farmer's in the Dell, the farmer's in the Dell,
    Heigh ho for Rowley oh, the farmer's in the Dell."

(Same wording till the dog is reached.)

"The dog wants a bone, the dog wants a bone,
    Heigh ho for Rowley oh, the dog wants a bone."

"The bone is left alone, the bone is left alone,
    Heigh ho for Rowley oh, the bone is left alone,"

when all retire as in the Tyrone version, leaving the young man in the centre to commence over again.

Thread the Needle.

"Open your gates as wide as high,
    And let King George's horses by;
    For the night is dark and we cannot see,
    But thread the long needle and sew."

This is a very ancient game.

Poor Woman of Sandyland.

"Here comes a poor woman from Sandyland,
    With all her children by the hand—
    One can knit and one can sew,
    And one can make a lily-white bow,
        Please take one in."

When all the children have been taken in, the old woman says:—

There was an old woman from Sandyland,
    With no children by the hand,
        Will you give me one?

The foregoing is from County Down, but Belfast has a localised version of its own called—

School Teacher.

"Here's a poor woman of Sandy Row,
    With all her children behind her;
One can knit and one can sew,
    And one can make a winder go.
      Please take one in.

Now poor [Nellie] she is gone,
    Without a farthing in her hand;
Nothing but a guinea gold ring.
      Good-bye, Nellie, good-bye!"

Both rhymes are corrupt forms or variants of an English singing game called "The Lady of the Land."

The line in the Sandy Row version "One can make a winder go," is an interesting reminiscence of the days of handloom weaving, when almost every house had its loom, and the task of winding the bobbins for the weaver's shuttle was usually allotted to the younger members of the family.

Queen Anne.

"Lady Queen Anne, she sits on a stand,
    She is fair as a lily, she is white as a swan;
A pair of green gloves all over her hand,
    She is the fairest lady in all the land.

Come taste my lily, come smell my rose,
    Which of my babes do you choose?
I choose not one, but I choose them all,
    So please Miss [Nell] give up the ball.

The ball is ours, it is not yours,
    We will go to the woods and gather flowers,
We will get pins to pin on clothes,
    You will get nails to nail your toes."

This is almost word for word as the rhyme is given in Chambers, except the two last lines, which in the Scots version are:—

"Cats and kittens bide within,
But we young ladies walk out and in."

Hugh Walpole in his fine novel, "Rogue Herries" (scene laid in Cumberland and Westmoreland; time, eighteenth century), makes Hugh Herries sing softly to himself "Lady Queen Anne" in practically the same words.

London Bridge.

London Bridge is broken down,
   Grant, said the little bee;
London Bridge is broken down,
   Where I'd be.

Stone and lime will build it up,
   Grant, said the little bee;
Stone and lime will build it up,
   Where I'd be.

Get a man to watch all night,
   Grant, said the little bee;
Get a man to watch all night,
   Where I'd be.

Perhaps the man might fall asleep,
   Grant, said the little bee;
Perhaps the man might fall asleep,
   Where I'd be.

Get a dog to watch all night,
   Grant, said the little bee;
Get a dog to watch all night,
   Where I'd be.

If that dog should run away,
   Grant, said the little bee;
If that dog should run away,
   Where I'd be.

Give that dog a bone to pick,
  Grant, said the little bee;
Give that dog a bone to pick,
  Where I'd be."

The above is quite different from the official version to be found in "Halliwell's Nursery Rhymes"—"London Bridge is broken down. Dance over my Lady Lee." Another form of the Irish version has "Grand, says the little Dee."

Nuts in May.

"Here we come gathering nuts in May,
  Nuts in May, nuts in May;
Here we come gathering nuts in May,
  May, May, May.

Who will you have for nuts in May?
Nuts in May, nuts in May;
Who will you have for nuts in May,
  May, May, May?

[Bessie Stewart] for nuts in May,
Nuts in May, nuts in May;
[Bessie Stewart] for nuts in May,
  May, May, May.

Very well, very well, so you may,
So you may, so you may;
Very well, very well, so you may,
  May, may, may.

Whom will you have to take her away,
Take her away, take her away?
Whom will you have to take her away,
  Way, way, way?

[Johnnie Brown] to take her away,
Take her away, take her away?
[Johnnie Brown] to take her away,
  Way, way, way.

With the exception of the "Mulberry Bush," this probably is the most widely played and popular of any singing game.

A game in which love-making does not form the staple ingredient is

The Wee Falorey Man.

"I'm the wee Falorey Man,
　　A rantin' rovin' Irishman,
I do all the work I can,
　　Follow the wee Falorey Man."

The leader performs certain actions and the others have to imitate him. This is also an English and Scottish game of which there are at least two versions under the name of "The Wee Melodie Man," but the words differ slightly from above, hence it has been set down here. Another rhyme that used to be in great vogue is:—

"Here is one knight has come from Spain,
　A courting of your daughter Jane—
　My daughter Jane she is too young,
　She can't abide your flattering tongue—
　Go home, you saucy knight,
　And scour your spurs till they grow bright.
　My spurs, my spurs, they owe you nought,
　For in your land they were not bought—
　Then fare you well, my lady gay,
　I'll go and court some other way.
　Come back! come back! you Spanish knight,
　And choose the one you love so bright."

There is a Scottish version called "We are three Jews" in which three Hebrew gentlemen take the place of the "Spanish Knight." It is much longer, but the Jews do not make so picturesque or suitable a figure as the adventurous Spaniard.

The following is another Irish form of which the writer has notes of from Tyrone in the north and Waterford in the south.

"Here are three tribes come down from Spain
To call upon my sister Jane;
My sister Jane she is too young
She can't abide your flattering tongue.

The fairest lily that I can see,
Is pretty little [Lizzie], will you come with me?

No!
The dirty little thing, she won't come out,
She won't come out, she won't come out;
The dirty little thing she won't come out
    To help us with our dancing.

Yes!
Now we've got a pretty maid, a pretty maid,
Now we've got a pretty maid
    To help us with our dancing.

CHAPTER IV.

Further singing games; their different versions.

Round About the Punch Bowl.

"Round about the punch bowl, punch bowl, punch bowl,
Round about the punch bowl, one, two, three.

First time never to fall, never to fall, never to fall,
First time never to fall, one, two, three.

Second time, catching time, catching time, catching time,
Second time, catching time, one, two, three.

Third time, kissing time, kissing time, kissing time
Third time, kissing time, one, two, three."

The foregoing is a Belfast version, and the following is a County Louth version which probably represents the oldest form of the rhyme:—

"Round about the punch bowl, one, two, three,
Open the gates and let the bride through.

Half a crown to know his name, to know his name, to know his name,
Half a crown to know his name, on a cold and frosty morning.

Ah! [Michael Andrews] is his name, is his name, is his name,
[Michael Andrews] is his name, on a cold and frosty morning.

Half a crown to know her name, to know her name, to know her name,
Half a crown to know her name, on a cold and frosty morning.

[Annie Keenan] is her name, is her name, is her name,
[Annie Keenan] is her name, on a cold and frosty morning.

They'll be married in the morning,
Round about the punch bowl, I." (? Hi!).

In County Down a different version is to be found:—

"Round about the punch bowl, one, two, three,
The last time they catch in time they'll not catch me.
[Lizzie] made a pudding nice and sweet,
Saying "taste love, taste love, don't say nay,
For next Sunday to church we will go,
Rings on her fingers and bells on her toes.
With her baby on her knee through the world she goes
Up the heathery mountain and down the rushy glen,
We darena go a hunting for fear of little men."

In the last six lines we have a mixture of three different rhymes. Farther south from Newry to Dublin, they have what is probably the original version but played in the same way. The making of the pudding is interesting, for in savage weddings in some parts of the world, the making by the bride of some dish, of which the bridegroom partakes, is a very important part of the marriage ceremony. It is called:—

Up the Heathery Mountain.

"Up the heathery mountain and down the rushy glen
We daren't go a hunting for Corner and his men.
We are all sally-butchers but one game cock.
And that's lovely [Johnnie], the flower of the flock.
He's the flower of the flock, he's the keeper of the glen,
He courted [Annie Nelson] before he was a man.
He hugged her, he cuddled her, he took her on his knee,
Saying, my dear [Annie], won't you marry me?
[Annie] made a pudding so nice and so sweet,
And [Johnnie] got his knife and cut it round and neat
Saying, taste love, taste love, don't say nay,
He hips and he clips and he buys her a ring,
A cherry for a church, and a gay gold ring."

Clara M. Patterson, Proc., Belfast, N.F.C., (1893-4, p. 52).

It was the two first lines of this folk rhyme that gave the suggestion to William Allingham for his famous poem, "The Fairies," a poem that is known wherever the English language is spoken, and without which no anthology of children's poetry would be complete. In the foreword to "Irish Songs and Poems" (2nd Ed., 1893) he says:

"Nor are the Fairies merely fantastic. Their quaint and tender mythology was round his cradle, in everybody's memory, in the faith (secretly and shyly) of some; nor is it yet extinct among the lonely crags and glens of Donegal."

> "Up the airy mountain,
>   Down the rushy glen,
> We daren't go a hunting
>   For fear of little men;
> Wee folk, good folk,
>   Trooping all together,
> Green jacket, red cap,
>   And white owl's feather."

The original of the words of the singing game which William Allingham turned to such good purpose are to be found in an old Scottish Jacobite song, "Charlie is my Darling." In the life of Scott, Vol. VII., p. 357, Sir Walter quotes the last four lines of the first set of words to the air, probably from memory as they are not quite correct. In Hogg's "Jacobite Relics," Vol. II., pp. 92-94, both sets of words are given but the historical interest of the last four lines has been completely spoilt by some busybody of an adapter. The correct original words will be found in "Jacobite Melodies." (Glasgow, 1825).

> "It's up yon heathery mountain,
>   And down yon scraggy glen,
> We darena gang a milking
>   For Charlie and his men."

Round About the Ladies.

> "Marching round the ladies, marching round the ladies,
> Marching round the ladies, as you have done before.

In and out the windows, in and out the windows,
In and out the windows, as you have done before.

Stand and face your lover, stand and face your lover,
Stand and face your lover, as you have done before.

Follow him (or her) to London, follow him to London,
Follow him to London, as you have done before.

Chase him back to Belfast, chase him back to Belfast,
Chase him back to Belfast, as you have done before."

This is a variant of the well-known rhyme, "Round about the Village."

Poor Toby is Dead.

"Poor Toby is dead and he lies in his grave,
He lies in his grave, he lies in his grave;
They planted an apple-tree over his head,
Over his head, over his head.

The apples grew ripe and beginning to fall,
Beginning to fall, beginning to fall;
The apples grew ripe and beginning to fall,
Beginning to fall, beginning to fall.

There came an old woman picking them up,
Picking them up, picking them up;
Poor Toby rose and gave her a kick,
Gave her a kick, gave her a kick.

And the poor old woman went hipperty hop,
Hipperty hop, hipperty hop;
And the poor old woman went hipperty hop."

For the conclusion of this series of Irish children's playing rhymes has been reserved the very fine one called "Jenny Jo," and sometimes "Jenny Jones," but, undoubtedly the correct and original form was "Jenny jo." Jo, in the Scottish dialect means sweetheart, and has been immortalised by Robert Burns in that unrivalled poem of wedded affection, "John Anderson, my jo."

In response to a request by Mrs. Gomme in "Notes and Queries" (7th Ser. XII. 367) for help in collecting children's singing games, the late W. H. Patterson sent in to "N & Q" the following version in which the game has been so graphically and charmingly described that to re-write it would be to spoil it.

Jenny Jo.

"In playing this game the children form themselves into two parties. The first consists of Jenny with her father and mother. Jenny, who is a very small child, is concealed behind her parents. All the other children form the party of suitors. The suitors retire some little distance off, and then approach Jenny's "house," singing:—

> We've come to court Jenny Jo,
> Jenny Jo, Jenny Jo;
> We've come to court Jenny Jo,
> Is she within?

Something tragic has happened, but the father and mother wish to temporise, so they sing in answer:—

> Jenny Jo's washing clothes,
> Washing clothes, washing clothes;
> Jenny Jo's washing clothes,
> You can't see her to-day.

The visiting party, who are holding hands, retire slowly, walking backwards, while all sing:—

> So fare ye well, ladies,
> O ladies, O ladies;
> So fare ye well, ladies,
> And gentlemen too.

The suitors return immediately, singing as before, and this is repeated a number of times; each time they receive an excuse that Jenny is "drying clothes," "starching clothes," "ironing clothes," till at last the afflicted parents are forced to announce the sad fact that:—

> Jenny Jo's lying dead,
> Lying dead, lying dead;
> Jenny Jo's lying dead,
> You can't see her to-day.

And then they add:—

> So turn again, ladies,
> O ladies, O ladies,
> So turn again, ladies,
> And gentlemen too.

But instead of returning to their own homes, the suitors remain and sing:—

> What shall we dress her in?
> Dress her in, dress her in?
> What shall we dress her in?
> Shall it be red?

Then the unhappy parents answer:—

> Red's for the soldiers,
> The soldiers, the soldiers;
> Red's for the soldiers,
> And that will not do.

Various other colours are suggested in song, but are found unsuitable—black, because "black's for the mourners," green, because "green's for the croppies," orange, because "orange is for the orangemen," and so on, until white is named, when the parents sing:—

> White's for the dead people,
> The dead people, the dead people,
> White's for the dead people,
> And that will just do.

Then the father and mother step aside, and Jenny is seen, lying quite still; a hush falls on the little party; the funeral must be arranged, when suddenly Jenny comes to life again and springs up, when the play ends with wild rejoicings."

In a County Down version instead of Jenny coming to life they make a funeral procession, the two biggest making a seat with their hands for "Jennie" and carrying her, followed by the rest in pairs, singing:—

> "We have lost a soldier, a soldier, a soldier,
> We have lost a soldier, and the king has lost a man.
> We will bury him in the bed of glory, glory, glory,
> We will bury him in the bed of glory,
> And we'll never see him any more."

CHAPTER V.

Children's school games and rhymes; tongue twisters; schoolboy spelling; Xmas games.

For small children, especially boys, there is no more popular game than touch, or "Tig," as it is generally called. These games are mostly started by a simple rhyme repeated by one of the players pointing to each of those engaged in the game, as he pronounces each word, and the player with whom the last word ends has the "tig." A characteristic one is:—

> "Mrs. Mason broke a basin,
> How much will it be?
> Half a crown, leave it down,
> Out goes she (or he)."

Another common one is:—

> "Eeny, meeny, miney mo,
> Catch a fellow by the toe,
> If he hollers let him go—
> Eeny, meeny, miney mo."

What seems a variant of the foregoing is:—

> "Eeny, meeny, figgety fig,
> Ill doll allymalig—
> Blockety block, stony rock,
> Hum, bum, thrush."

In both England and Scotland there are numerous similar jumbles of nonsense used as counting out rhymes.

A popular couplet used by boys when starting races is:—

> "Bell horses! bell horses, what time o' day?
> One o'clock, two o'clock, three and away."

This is common in England where in some parts they have an

additional couple of lines:—

> "The master is coming, and what will he say?
> He'll whip them, and drive them, and send them away."

The origin of this rhyme was that in olden days merchandise was transported on the backs of pack horses. At that time there were only narrow roads or bridle paths and the leading horse carried ear-bells on his bridle. Later the leading horse of a waggon team carried a set of from five to eight bells, housed on his collar. This was necessary to warn an approaching team or train coming from the opposite direction. Ear-bells were of hemispherical form and in Ireland termed *nodals*.

Cutchie Cutchoo.

A child's game that was in vogue in Ireland in the latter part of the eighteenth, and early part of the nineteenth century. The players bent themselves into a posture as near sitting down as possible— what is known as "hunkering down," the girls with their clothes tucked between their knees, and one chases the others in a hopping motion, the feet kept together, crying "catch you, catch you!" The slurring of the words in pronouncing them quickly gave its name to the game, the rhyme of which is as follows:—

> "Cutchie cutchoo, grannie, your bread's a burning,
> Cutchie cutchoo, it's ready for turning."

Whereupon grannie cries, "then turn it."

Whoever kept up the hopping longest was the winner.

A similar game was played in Scotland under the name of "Curcuddie," but had a different rhyme, and in the north of Scotland it was known as "Harry Hurcheon."

Time glides on, and the child when sent to school very soon finds that:—

> "Multiplication's my vexation,
>   Division's twice as bad,
> The Rule of Three it puzzles me,
>   But Fractions drive me mad.

> Tare and Tret it makes me fret,
> And makes me curse and swear,
> And the master pull my hair."

Of course it was a boy whose mathematical studies provoked such an outburst, girls never, never complain, but are always nice and gentle however trying "them ould sums" may be. Meanwhile the time was not always occupied over difficult problems in arithmetic, prepared by teachers just for the purpose of tormenting boys and making them unhappy. There were rhymes in keeping with his advanced status as a schoolboy, perhaps not always strictly grammatical, such as:—

> "One, two, buckle my shoe,
> Three, four, my coat's tore,
> Five, six, a bundle of sticks,
> Seven, eight, lay them straight,
> Nine, ten, a fine fat hen,
> Eleven, twelve, roast her well,
> Thirteen, fourteen, bend a bow,
> Fifteen, sixteen, shoot a crow,
> Seventeen, eighteen, the crow's dead,
> Nineteen, twenty, hit him on the head."

Then perhaps if the teacher turns his (or her) back for a moment, as even the teachers in the very best schools find occasion to do sometimes, I am informed, he will say to his neighbour:—

> "Nievy, navy, nick nack,
> Which hand will ye tak'?
> The right or the wrang,
> I'll beguile you if I can." (Co. Antrim.)

The rhyme is used in a game played with closed hands; in one hand of the player is a marble, or any small object, the other is empty. The second player tries to choose the hand that encloses the object, and in case of missing pays a forfeit.

Halliwell, in "Popular Rhymes," gives this as an old English game that goes by the name of "Handy Dandy."

An unsuspecting newcomer would perhaps be requested to:—

> "Put your finger in the crow's nest, the crow's not at home,
>   She's gone to Ballygawley to pick a white stone,"

at the same time forming an open square with his first and second fingers. Should the other party be innocent of the trick and comply, the inserted finger is immediately held fast and severely pinched by the thumb underneath, while the pincher exclaims "the crow's come back!"

Or, perhaps it would be:—

> "Holly and hazel went to the wud (wood),
>   Holly brought hazel home by the lug,"

suiting the action to the word.

In the north of Ireland if the boy felt at all nearly a match for his tormentor, he was likely to present his shut fist and say:—

> "There's your bread, and there's your butter,
>   And there's the fist can give you your supper."

In Tipperary it used to be when boys fell out they vowed eternal enmity as follows:—

> "By the back of my hand and sole of my shoe,
>   I'll never speak again to you."

Or perhaps some one has offended, wilfully or otherwise, and says:—

> "I beg your pardon."
> "I grant your grace,
>   I beg the cat to spit in your face,"

returns the indignant one.

In case of a desk or form being rather crowded, somebody would say:—

> "Two little tailors came from Tuam,
>   And all they wanted was elbow-room,"

at the same time striking out with the elbows.

In Dublin it ran:—

"There was an old cobbler that lived in the Coombe,
And all that he wanted was elbow room."

The Coombe is a very thickly populated district in the heart of the city.

Then if any boy or girl who had red hair gave offence they were saluted with:—

"Red head, fiery skull,
Every hair of your head would tether a bull."

Every intelligent schoolboy also knew that on:—

"Saturday night my wife she died,
On Sunday she was buried,
Monday was my roving day,
And Tuesday I got married;
Wednesday I stole a cow,
And Thursday I was taken,
Friday I was condemned to die,
And Saturday I was hung up like bacon."

This made a fairly crowded week, and the hero must surely have been glad of a rest, even in a coffin.

There is a case on record that may have been the original of the rhyme. "At Lanark, in Scotland, Elizabeth Fairy was proclaimed (in order to marriage) on Sunday, January 31st, 1736; married on Monday; gave birth to a child on Tuesday; her husband stole a horse on Wednesday, for which he was banished on Thursday; the issue of the marriage died on Friday and was interred on Saturday—all in one week." (*Notes and Queries*, Jan.-June, 1861, p. 391).

A very similar Renfrewshire rhyme runs:—

"Tom married a wife on Monday,
He cut a stick on Tuesday,
He beat her well on Wednesday,
Sick she was on Thursday,
Dead she was on Friday.
Glad was Tom on Saturday
To bury his wife on Sunday."

CHAPTER VI.

Children's school games and rhymes; tongue twisters; schoolboy spelling; Xmas games.

When a new pupil came to the school one of the first questions asked by his classmates was sure to be "What do they call you?"

Now, if he had been properly trained at his previous school, he would promptly reply

> "Patchey Dawley."
> "What's your name?"
> "Butter and crame (cream),"

to which his interrogator would answer "A very good name for winter."

In England they have the rhyme somewhat different.

> "What's your name?
> Pudding of Thame;
> If you ask me again I'll tell you the same."

Southey's *Doctor*, p. 351, one volume edition, contains amongst other odd names of the foul fiend, that of "Pudding of Thame," to which the author simply adds parenthetically "fie on such pudding."

The newcomer had made a very good commencement, but it might be no harm to test him a little further, and accordingly the riddle would be propounded to him:—

> "Jack and John, and young Nip On,
> Went down to the river to bathe;
> Jack and John were drowned,
> And which of them was saved?"

If he were unwary, the newcomer answered—"Nip On," upon which those adjacent proceeded to take him at his word and pinch him black and blue.

The formula for asking for something was:—

> "Fill a pot, fill a pan,
> Fill a poor blind man's han'."

Then under other circumstances it was:—

> "Shake hands brother,
> You're a rogue and I'm another,
> You stole beef and I stole bone,
> You'll go to jail and I'll stay at home."

Schoolboys had also tongue-twisters of their own as:—

> "A wee, ree-ra-rough-cut bunet sow,
> Had three wee, ree-ra-rough cut bunet pigs,
> Commit my cut, my bunty cut."

There are a number of rhymes in vogue with the schoolchildren, such as:

> "Hail, rain, frost and snow,
> Pay the rent or out you go."

This had its origin in the condition of tenant farmers in bygone days, a state of affairs now happily at an end. Vivid pictures of those times in Ulster will be found in William Carleton's "Tubber Derg" (*Traits and Stories*), also in "The Emigrants of Aghadara," and "Valentine M'Clutchy," while C. J. Kickham has done the same for Munster in "Knocknagow, or the homes of Tipperary," and "Sally Cavanagh."

Another rhyme which the writer picked up in County Tyrone when a boy was:—

> "When I was a lad I lived with my dad,
> And I jumped into a bean swad (pod);
> The bean swad it was too full,
> So I jumped into a roaring bull;
> The roaring bull he was too fat,
> So I jumped into a gentleman's hat;
> The gentleman's hat it was too fine,
> So I jumped into a bottle of wine;
> The bottle of wine it was too clear,

So I jumped into a barrel of beer;
The barrel of beer it was too thick,
So I jumped into an oak stick;
The oak stick began to crack,
And I fell on my back."

This belongs to the cumulative class of rhymes and stories, of which "Kid, kid, go over the bridge." and "The House that Jack built" are classical examples, as well as the folk tale, "I'll be wiser the next time," in Kennedy's "Legendary Fictions of the Irish Celts," and "The Unlucky Messenger," in "The Fireside Stories of Ireland." Schoolboys also had a code of spelling of their own that was not to be found in Sullivan's "Spelling Book Superseded." Lombe Atthill, in "Recollections of an Irish Doctor," p. 55, gives an example:—

"A knife and a clod spells Nebby Cod,
A knife and a razor Nebby Cod Nazer.
One pair of boots and two pair of shoes
Spells Nebby Cod Nazer, the King of the Jews."

Another favourite word for spelling in the north of Ireland was "Widow Deruffy." W, double o, double d, y, ruph-ruff, and i p h f i. Then there were many other simple words spelled in a way unknown to Sullivan, such as o.f. a noggin of broth; i.n. a potato skin; o.u.t, a potato scout. While in each district schoolboys spelled place names in a fashion undreamt of by topographers. Two or three examples will serve. 'Two sticks stannin' spells Dungannon; 'a man and a boy' spells Aughnacloy: 'two men wheelin' spells New Zealan', etc.

In bygone times it was a favourite amusement for children to collect pins at Christmastime to use as stakes, the games being played by spinning a teetotum or by guessing. The following rhyme was used in guessing. One of the players took a pin and placing his hands behind his back, concealed the pin in one of them, then holding out his hands in front, the other player pointing alternately to each hand thus held, repeated:—

"Pippety, poppety, play me a pin,
Open the door and let me in,

> Let me lose or let me win,
> This is the hand the pin lies in."

If the hand that he pointed to when saying the last word of the rhyme held the pin the rhymer won it—if not, he paid a pin as forfeit. Where this game was too slow for sporting characters there was a quicker way of winning or losing pins. One player concealed a number of pins in his hand and said:—

> "Peep at the bush."
> "I'll break your smush," was the reply.
> "How many times?"

If the reply was correct the guesser won, if not, an equal number of pins were forfeited.

The teetotum used in playing has four sides marked respectively A.T.P.N., and according to which side falls uppermost the spinner wins or loses. As the boys' rhyme has it:—

> "A. for all, T. take up,
> P. put down, N. for Nicholas Nothing."

Amongst the boys' games that have fallen into disuse was one named "Brogey More," which was sung to the beautiful old Irish air, "The Rose Tree," to which Thomas Moore set the words, "I'd mourn the hopes that leave me."

The game was played as follows:—One boy stood with his back to the wall, a second one stooped and placed his head against the other one's chest, while all the rest stood round the stooping boy. Each was given a name which was rather picturesque, such as "Brogey More," "Singey Gore," "Oul' Grey Rat," "Pot an' Pan," etc., etc.

The origin of these names is unknown. Having all been named the leader started the following doggerel rhyme, the others all joining in and singing to the tune mentioned:—

> Lay on him Brogey More,"
> With yer fa-re-a-raddy O!
> And likewise "Singey Gore,"
> With yer fa-re-a-raddy O!

Whilst this was going on, the boys were "laying on," with their fists on the back of the stooping boy, and keeping time to the music. The game was to puzzle the players as to when to lay on and leave off, and the one named had to be on the alert that he made no mistake, for if he did he had to pay a penalty of taking the place of the stooping boy. The rhyme went on:—

> Lay on him "Pot an' Pan,"!
> With yer fa-re-a-raddy O!
> Take off him every one,
> With yer fa-re-a-raddy O!

> Lay on him "Oul' Gray Rat,"
> With yer fa-re-a-raddy O!
> Take off him "Brogey More,"
> With yer fa-re-a-raddy O!

> Lay on him "Brogey More,"
> With yer fa-re-a-raddy O!
> And likewise "Singey Gore,"
> With yer fa-re-a-raddy O!

> Lay on him "Pot an' Pan,"
> With yer fa-re-a-raddy O!

Another boys' game that used to be played was "Hurley Burley."

This was also played by one boy standing with his back against the wall, another stoops and puts his head against his chest, another takes his place behind the stooping boy, while the leader recites the following rhyme:—

> "Hurley, Burley! trumpa trace;
> The cow ran from the market place,
> Some go far and some go near—
> Where shall this poor Frenchman steer?"

The stooping boy tells him to go to "Paddy Gaw's Corner." The Frenchman then goes to his station, about fifty yards distant. The same ceremony is gone through and another boy is sent to "Wilson's Grocery"; another up "Eakin's Entry," and so on till all the boys have been sent to different stations. The leader then shouts—"Are you all in your places?"

Waiting a moment for their reply, he then calls out, "Hurley home; hurley home; hurley home." The race then commences as to who shall get home first. The last one in has to pay a penalty, and so he is surrounded, and each one taking a lock of his hair, all repeat together:—

> "Rannell him, Dick;
> Catch him, Davey,
> All the men, three score and ten,
> Anyone not at the rannelling match
> Will be rannelled over again;
> Heigh ho, buttermilk, oh!
> Short pluck, or long draw?"

The unfortunate victim answers "short pluck," when his tormentors give his hair a pluck and he is released.

This is a Belfast variant of "How many horns stand up?" given at p. 400 of "English Folk-Rhymes," by G. F. Northall.

CHAPTER VII.

Christmas Rhymers.

" 'Tis a pleasant thing, in these Christmas times,
   To meet quaint stories in garrulous rhymes—
   Pleasant to read of our forefathers' ways,
   In our great-great grandfathers' days."
                                        Kishoge Papers, No. 10.

In the north of Ireland as Christmas drew near it was customary to get up a company of Rhymers who went round the shops and private dwellings reciting their rhymes and collecting money. These were the latter day descendants of the mummers of olden times, who at times of festivity played their pranks for the amusement of their fellows as well as their own. They dressed up in such fantastic costumes as they could manage, and represented various characters, such as St. George, Oliver Cromwell, Beelzebub, Devil Doubt, the Doctor, etc. Each had a rhyme to recite about himself, which he did with such intonation and gestures as he considered appropriate.

Lombe Atthill, in his "Recollections of an Irish Doctor" (pp. 53-54) thus describes the advent of the Christmas Rhymers at his father's house in county Fermanagh in the first half of the nineteenth century.

". . . the excitement of us children, when the servant would, some evening between Christmas and Twelfth Night, enter the drawing-room and utter the almost magic words, "The mummers have come." Down we would rush to find the kitchen cleared, the servants ranged round the wall, and the table brought to one end for us to stand on. These mummers were boys, farmers' and labourers' sons residing in the district, and were of course poorly clad, but decorated with scraps of coloured calico and ribbon sewed on here and there, and I think they wore paper caps of various shapes. They came into the kitchen one by one, each reciting some scrap of doggerel verse, and when the whole band had come in they danced in some fantastic way upon the kitchen floor. Then a little money being given to them, they went their way to some farmer's house, at which they might hope to receive a trifle. One of their rhymes has fixed itself in my memory, probably because it frightened me. A boy, aged about thirteen, rather better got up than the others, with a frying-pan in his hand, on one occasion entered, strutted into the centre of the floor, and turning to face us, said:—

> "Here come I, little Devil Doubt;
> Under my arm I carry a clout;
> In my hand a dripping-pan;
> Money I want and money I crave,
> If you don't give me money, I sweep all to the grave."

These mummeries, like many other old customs, have disappeared since the famine years."

Omnes:—

> Room, room, brave gallant boys—
> Give us room to rhyme;
> We have come to show our activity
> At this Christmas time.
> Active youth and active age,
> The like was never acted on a stage;
> And if you don't believe what I say,
> Enter in, St. George, and clear the way.

St. George:—

> Here comes I, St. George, from England have I sprung,
> One of those noble deeds of valour to begin.
> Seven long years in a close cave have I been kept,
> And out of that into a prison leapt,
> And out of that into a block of stone,
> Where I made many a sad and grievous moan.
> Many a giant did I subdue,
> I ran the fiery dragon through and through—

> I fought them all courageously,
> And still will always fight for liberty,
> Here I draw my bloody weapon;
> Show me the man that dare me stand,
> I'll cut him down with my courageous hand.

The Turkish Knight:—

A youth with blackened face here steps forward and says to him:—

> "I am the man that dare you challenge,
> Whose courage is great,
> And with my sword I made dukes and earls to quake."

St. George:—

"Who are you but a poor silly lad?"

The Turkish Knight replies:—

> "I am a Turkey champion, from Turkeyland I came,
> To fight you, great George by name;
> I'll cut you and slash you, and send you to Turkey,
> To make mince pies baked in an oven,
> And after I have done I'll fight e'er a champion in Christendom."

Here St. George sticks him with his sword. Having done this he shouts:—

> "A doctor, a doctor! Ten pounds for a doctor!
> Is there never a doctor to be found who can
> Cure this man of his deep and mortal wound?"

A doctor dressed up in top hat, and with a bottle of medicine in his hand, comes forward and recites:—

> "Here comes I, old Doctor Brown,
> The best old doctor in the town;
> I am a doctor pure and good,

> And with my sword I'll staunch his blood.
> If you've a mind his life to save
> Full fifty guineas I must have."

St. George asks him:—

"What can you cure, doctor?"

The Doctor answers:—

> "I can cure the plague within, the plague without,
> The palsy or the gout,
> Moreover than that," sez he,
> "If you bring me an old woman of threescore and ten,
> And the knuckle bone of her toe be broken,
> I can fix it again.
> And if you don't believe what I say,
> Enter St. Patrick and clear the way."

St. Patrick:—

> "Here comes I, St. Patrick, in shining armour bright,
> A famous champion and a worthy knight.
> What was St. George but St. Patrick's boy,
> Who fed his horse with oats and hay,
> And afterwards he ran away."

St. George:—

> G.—I say by St. George, you lie, sir,
> P.—Pull out your sword and try, sir,
> G.—Pull out your purse and pay, sir,
> P.—I'll run my sword through your body,
> And make you run away, sir.
> So enter in, Oliver Cromwell, and clear the way.

Oliver Cromwell:—

> "Here comes I, Oliver Cromwell, as you may suppose

I've conquered many nations with my long copper nose,
I've made my foes to tremble and my enemies for to quake,
And I've beat my opposers till I've made their hearts to ache;
And if you don't believe what I say,
Enter Beelzebub and clear the way."

Beelzebub:—

"Here comes I, Beelzebub,
And over my shoulder I carry my club,
And in my hand a dripping-pan,
I think myself a jolly old man;
And if you don't believe what I say,
Enter Devil Doubt and clear the way."

Devil Doubt:—

"Here comes I, wee Devil Doubt,
If you don't give me money I'll sweep you all out—
Money I want, and money I crave,
If you don't give me money I'll sweep you all to your grave."

The Leader:—

"Ladies and Gentlemen—Since our sport is ended,
Our box must now be recommended;
Our box would speak if it had a tongue—
Nine or ten shillings would do it no wrong,
All silver, no brass; bad ha'pence won't pass."

Exit the Company.

Sung by them all:—

"Your cellar doors are locked,
And we are like to choke,
And it's all for the drink
That we sing, boys, sing."

The words of the Christmas Rhyme as printed have been compiled from two slightly different versions, occasional words or lines missing in either being supplemented by the other, so as to make it as complete as possible. One copy used is a little chap book printed by Nicholson, Church Lane, Belfast, about 1880, illustrated by rough woodcuts. A facsimile of it was presented as a supplement with "The Irish Book Lover," for July-December. 1928. The editor in his note on it says:—"The type and borders are fairly modern, certainly not older than 1850, but the woodcuts may date back a full two hundred years.

The play itself seems from recollection to be a survival in debased form of the mystery play of **The Seven Champions of Christendom**."

The other set of words came from the Ballymoney district (north Antrim) and is printed by the late Sir John Byers in his "Sayings, Proverbs, and Humour of Ulster," Belfast, 1904.

In a very imperfect version taken down from oral recitation by R. S. Lepper, Carnalea, county Down, in 1913, and printed in "Notes and Queries" (11th Ser. VIII.. pp. 81-83) there is a further verse:—

[Enter little Johnny Conny.]

Little Johnny Conny:—

"Here comes I, little Johnny Conny,
I'm the man that carries the money,
Big long pockets down to my knees,
Holds two bob bits and two bawbees.[5]
All silver, no brass, bad ha'pence won't pass."

There is a full account of the county Wexford Christmas Rhymers in Patrick Kennedy's "Banks of the Boro," pp. 227-231. In it the words and characters are very similar to those already given. The principal difference being that the mummers would not soil their consequence by taking up a collection. At the manor house or large farmhouse which they visited, after the play was over the evening was wound up by a dance kept up till a tolerably late hour—the fiddler being in all cases paid by the performers who never received any recompense beyond the hospitality extended to them by their hosts.

Sir Walter Scott in Note P. to "The Pirate," gave the words used as a prelude to the sword dance performed by the Zetlanders, the characters being the **Seven Champions of Christendom**. The words have a considerable resemblance to the Irish rhyme.

Christmas Mummers seem to have performed over the greater part of the British Isles. The play dates back to the Crusades, say about the twelfth century or thereabouts and seems to be the only survival of the pre-Reformation folk drama. A full account of it in England is given by R. J. E. Tidley, under the title of "The Mummer's Play."

CHAPTER VIII.

Two Tyrone versions of Christmas Rhyme.

The following rhyme comes from the west side of Tyrone, the district lying between Fintona, Dromore and Trillick. It differs very considerably from the county Antrim and county Down versions. It was acted within the last couple of years and is probably acted still. The writer is indebted for the words to a Tyrone friend, happily having a kindred interest with himself in the folklore of his native county.

County Tyrone Christmas Rhyme

Enter Father Christmas.

> I wish you all a merry Christmas, and a prosperous New Year;
> With pocketfulls of money, and barrelfulls of beer.
> Room, boys, room there; give us room to rhyme,
> We'll show you something funny about this Christmas time.
> Active youth and active age:
> The like was never seen on any stage.
> If you don't believe the words I say,
> Come in, Jack Straw, and he will clear the way."

Enter Jack Straw. (All dressed in straw.)

> "Here comes me, Jack Straw,
>   Such a man you never saw:
>   Through a rock, through a reel,
>   Through an oul' spinnin' wheel:
>   Through a bag of pepper,
>   Through a miller's hopper:
>   Through a sheep's shin bone,
>   Such a man was never known.
>   If you don't believe the words I say,
>   Come in, wee Divil Doubt, an' he will clear the way."

———•◆•———

53

Enter wee Divil Doubt:—

> "Here comes me, wee Divil Doubt,
> If you don't give me money I'll sweep you all out.
> Money I want, and money I crave;
> If you don't give me money I'll sweep you all to your grave.
> If you don't believe what I say,
> Come in, Fiddley Funny, an' he'll clear the way."

Enter Fiddley Funny:—

> "Here comes I, Fiddley Funny,
> I'm the man that lifts the money.
> Hub bub bees, down on my knees,
> With a little box under my arm,
> Three or four shillings will do me no harm,
> Five or six will do me some good.
> All silver, no brass; bad money won't pass.
> If you don't believe the words I say,
> Come in, Beelzebub, and he'll clear the way."

Enter Beelzebub:—

> "Here comes I, Beelzebub,
> And over my shoulder I carry my club;
> And in my hand a drippin' pan,
> I count myself a jolly good man.
> If you don't believe the words I say,
> Come in, Big Head, an' he'll clear the way."

Enter Big Head:—

> "Here comes me, that didn't come yet,
> With my big head and my little wit.
> Though my head is big and my body is small,
> I'll do my endeavour to plaze yiz all."

Enter the Clown with a sword and flourishes it about:—

"Now the performance is about to start: bumbussling and t'wisseling. Tossing and retossing. Them that comes in on their head goes out on their feet." General scuffle in which one of the company is struck with the clown's sword. There is a general cry of:—"A doctor! a doctor! Ten pounds for a doctor."

Enter the Doctor:—

Cries of "Doctor! doctor! what can you cure?"

Doctor:—

> "I can cure the plague within, the plague without,
> I can cure the ague or the gout.
> And any oul' woman with ten divils in,
> I can knock twelve divils out."

Here the Doctor restores the wounded man with some passes, and there is general rejoicing in which all burst into song to the strains of a fiddle. The whole ending up with an Irish step-dance.

Another Christmas rhyme which I am enabled to print through the kindness of a fellow Tyrone man, comes from the Donemana district, near Strabane, north Tyrone. It differs very considerably from the two preceding rhymes.

North Tyrone Christmas Rhyme.

First Player:—

> "Room, room, ye gallant boys, and give us room to rhyme,
> And we will show you some activity about the Christmas time.
> Active youth and active age, the like was never acted on a stage.
>   If you don't believe me what I say,
>   Enter Prince George and he will clear the way."

Prince George:—

> "Here comes I, Prince George, from England I have sprung,
> I have fought the fire through and through,
> I have fought the devil black and blue.
> England's right and Ireland's wrong
> Where is that man of arm strong,
> That I couldn't cut down with my precious sword, sir?"

First Player:—

Pull out your purse and pay, sir.

Prince George:—

Pull out your sword and try, sir.

First Player:—

> I'll run my dagger through your heart,
> And make you die away, sir.

(Stabs at Prince George who falls.)

First Player:—

> Doctor! Doctor! Ten pounds for a doctor.
> Is there no doctor to be found to cure this deep and deadly
> wound?

Enter Doctor:—

> Yes, bedads, I am a doctor pure and true,
> With my broadsword I'll staunch his blood.
> If you want this man's life saved, fifty guineas I must have,
> sir.

First Player:—

When did you become a doctor?

Doctor:—

In my long travels.

First Player:—

Where did you travel from?

Doctor:—

> I travelled from Higerty Pigerty,
> Where the dead pigs run up and down the street,
> With knives and forks in their heart.
> I ran one stam, ram race, ate them all up in a gace,
> And that's what made my belly so big.

First Player:—

What can you cure, Doctor?

Doctor:—

> I can cure the plague within, the plague without, the palsy
> and the gout;
> Where there is nine devils in I can knock ten devils out,
> With the houzel of the hatchet or the brains of the wee
> creepy stool.

First Player:—

What is your plaster, Doctor?

Doctor:—

> Hen's pens, peesy weesy, midges' eyes, bum bees, bacon;
> The juice of the riddle, the sap of tongs,
> Three duck eggs nine yards long,
> All put in a bladder and stirred with a grey cat's feather.

Put in a jolly man's stocking soles as tight as he can thole,
Three weeks before the sun rises and a fortnight after she
    sets,
To spit as straight as a rush in the neck of a tuppenny bottle.
If that does not cure him the devil may cure him,
For I'll not cure him to-night, sir.

First Player:—

Doctor, cure him if you can.

Doctor:—

Oh! stop, stop! I have a little bottle in the waistband of my
    breeches,
Some call it this and some calls it that,
But I call it Hokeys Pokeys, Eleagant Panis;
Take three snuffs of this, Prince George, and rise and fight
    again, sir.

Prince George:—

Once I was dead, but now I'm alive,
Thanks, thanks to the Doctor who made me revive.
If you don't believe what I say,
Call in Beelzebub and he'll clear the way.

Beelzebub:—

Here comes I, Beelzebub,
And over my shoulder I carry my club,
In my hand a dripping pan,
I think myself a jolly old man.
Last Christmas night I turned the spit,
I burnt my finger and feel it yet.
Between my finger and my thumb
There rose a blister as big as a plum,

And it's not away yet.
I took out my pipe and began to smoke
Until the slavers (spittle) ran down the back of my coat.
Up jumps the cock sparrow and flew across the table.
Up jumps the wee pot and began to play with the ladle.
Up jumps the dish-cloth and all its dirty duds,
And up jumps the besom between the two lugs.
Up jumps the beetle saying can you not agree?
Send for Mick Murphy and bring him here to me.
When Mike Murphy came there he had a belly as big as a
    bear.
He ate a cow, he ate a bullock and a half;
He licked the ladle, swallowed the spoon,
And wasn't foo when a' was done.
If you don't believe me what I say,
Enter in, Oliver Cromwell, and he will clear the way.

Oliver Cromwell:—

Here comes I, Oliver Cromwell, as you may suppose,
I have conquered many nations with my long copper nose.
I made the Dutch to travel and the Spaniard to quake—
I fought the Dutchman until his both sides ached.
Samson was a good man but he couldn't conquer me.
If you don't believe what I say,
Enter in, Jack Straw, and he will clear the way.

Jack Straw:—

Here comes I, Jack Straw striddle,
Knocked be the dure through a riddle;
Through a rock, through a reel, through an ould spinning
    wheel;
Through an ould mill hopper, through an ould bag of paper;
Through an ould woman's puce: shank skin and bone.
If you don't believe me what I say,

Enter in, Big Head, and he will clear the way.

Big Head:—

Here comes I that never came yet,
Big Head and little wit.
The more my head's big, my body's small,
I do my best to please you all.
If you don't believe me what I say,
Enter the Wren, he will clear the way.

Wren:—

Here comes I, the king of all small birds,
The more I am small my family's great,
Rise up, you landlords, and give us a treat,
And if you treat us with the best,
I hope your souls may go to rest.
If you don't believe me what I say,
Enter wee Divil Doubt, he will clear the way.

Wee Divil Doubt (with a besom):—

Here comes I, wee Divil Doubt, with a rout, tout, tout.
If you don't give me money I'll sweep you all out,
For money I want and money I crave,
If you don't give me money I'll sweep you all to your grave.

All join in.

For we didn't come to your door to beg nor to borrow,
But we came to your door to drive away all sorrow.
With your pockets full of money and your barrels full of
beer,
We wish you a happy Christmas and a prosperous New Year.

The actors usually wore long white coats. Some, coats turned wrong side out, faces all made up and comic hats. Some were made by taking some corn (oats), tying the stalks and having the corn all over the face. Each could have the most striking rig-out that they were able to design or afford. For Wee Divil a heather besom is the usual equipment, and of course the Doctor has a bag and bottle. In the foregoing performance although she does not appear in the text, there was always a woman, or some one dressed up as one, who came in after the last song and gave a dance. Some one played a mouth-organ or whistled, after which she went round with the hat.

It will be noticed that there is a borrowing from the Wren Boys song in this unusual version.

The acting of this play was very widely spread. It was played in Scotland at the New Year under the name of "**Galatian**," and in some parts of the north of England as the "Christmas Tup," and in other districts as the "Derby Ram," of which a complete version is given in "Ballads and Songs of Derbyshire" (1867), while in the midlands and south of England it figures as "St. George and the Dragon." In 1571 according to Collier's "Annals of the Stage" (I. p. 7, note II. p. 148) the miracle play of St. George was acted at Basingbourne, and Halliwell (*Dictionary of Old English Plays*) mentions "St. George and the Dragon," a farce acted in Bartholomew Fair in the seventeenth century. It was also prevalent in Wales. In "Tales and Traditions of Tenby" (Pembrokeshire) published in 1858, there is a valuable chapter on the "Manners and Customs of the people of Tenby," in which the dialogue is given almost word for word with the north of Ireland version. It has also been noted in Cornwall and the Isle of Wight. This play was probably brought over to Ireland by both English and Scots settlers, and varies in different localities. One of the oldest mystery plays is "St. George and the Dragon," and eastern characters were probably introduced at the time of the Crusades.

There is a long article on "St. George, the Turkish Knight, etc.," in *Notes and Queries*, volume for July-December, 1878, pp. 484-489, and in the same journal, for 17th July, 1925, on "Christmas Mummers of Stoneleigh." The actors and action of the play differ somewhat from the Irish version, but many lines are the same in both. St. George has been modernised into King George.

In and around Belfast, from enquiries made, the custom appears to have been discontinued about the year 1870 or shortly after, but appears to have lingered on in some parts of the country, as until the year 1898 or '99, the Rhymers used to go round the town of Carrickfergus, visiting from house to house and collecting what pence they could during the days immediately before Christmas, and the writer heard of the Christmas Rhymers in Donaghadee as late as 1924. The custom had, however, got out of date, the townspeople did not encourage the performers, the authorities frowned upon them, and consequently the experiment has not been repeated. We fear that the old custom has died out in other localities where it was formerly prevalent, so that the Rhymers can no longer bid farewell to their patrons in the words:—

> "Hang out your silken handkerchief upon your golden spear,
> We'll come no more a-rhyming until another year."

CHAPTER IX.

The wren boys; the wren song; remote antiquity of the custom.

The practice of hunting the wren obtains not only over the south and west, but over a great part of Ireland. It is also followed at certain periods of the year in England, Wales, the Isle of Man, and the Continent.

It is, or was, the custom in parts of Pembrokeshire, on Twelfth Night (January 6th) to carry about a wren in a small house made of wood, with doors and windows decorated with ribbons, etc. If the serenaders had been fortunate in their hunting they sometimes had several wrens in the same house, which was carried round in similar fashion to the Irish procedure. The rhyme sung is given in "Notes and Queries." January-June, 1864 (pp. 109-110), and differs entirely from the Irish version. In the valuable chapter on the "Manners and Customs of the people of Tenby," in "Tales and Traditions of Tenby" (pp. 13-15), there is given the words and music of an altogether different rhyme. It is highly characteristic and runs to ten verses in all, of which we give as a specimen the first two: —

The Cutty Wren.

"O, where are you going? says the Milder (miller) to the
Melder (malster).
O, where are you going? says the younger to the elder.
O, I cannot tell, says Festel to Fose,
We're going to the woods, said John the Red Nose,
We're going to the woods, said John the Red Nose.

O, what will you do there? says the Milder to the Melder,
O, what will you do there? says the younger to the elder.
To shoot the Cutty Wren, said John the Red Nose,
To shoot the Cutty Wren, said John the Red Nose.

And so on until she is finally boiled "in brass pans and cauldrons."

In the "Isle of Man Times" for 2nd January, 1892, there is an account of the performance of the Wren Boys on St. Stephen's Day, and the report goes on to say "We were glad, however, to see that a great number of bushes were minus the wren itself."

Halliwell, in his "Nursery Rhymes" (2nd ed. 1843) gives at page 180 the English version of the "Hunting of the Wren" and at page 249 the Isle of Man "Hunting the Wren," which, according to this authority, used to take place on the 24th of December, though afterwards observed on St. Stephen's Day.

Why the harmless wren is disliked and hunted on St. Stephen's Day has never been satisfactorily accounted for. In the north-east counties the following complimentary rhyme is common amongst schoolboys:—

> "The wee Jenny Wren she lays sixteen,
> And brings them out both neat and clean.
> The scabby cuckoo, she lays but two,
> And brings them out with enough to do,"

which may be a compliment to the wren, but is poor natural history.

There are several versions of the reason why the wren is disliked by the southern Irish, all of them equally apocryphal. The earliest is that in ancient times when the native Irish were about to catch their Danish enemies asleep, a wren perched upon a drum and awoke the invader's sentinels just in time to save the whole army. Next, the wren's performance was transferred to the saving of a portion of Cromwell's army, and later on it is a portion of the army of William of Orange, for all of which no foundation in history can be traced, in fact for so tiny a bird as the wren to make a noise upon a drum is such a physical impossibility that it would be wasting time to discuss the subject.

Whatever the origin of the custom, however, it is still kept up in the south and west of Ireland, and the writer has heard of it as far north as the counties of Cavan, Leitrim and Donegal. Lady Wilde, in "Ancient Legends of Ireland" (p. 58) places the drum legend in Cromwell's time, and then goes on to say "So ever since the Irish hunt the wren on St. Stephen's Day and teach their children to run it through with thorns whenever it can be caught. A dead wren was also tied to a pole and carried from house to house by boys who demanded money. If nothing was given the wren was buried at the doorstep, which was considered a great insult to the family, and a great degradation." A further light is thrown on Lady Wilde's notice of the Wren-boys by a note in the "Journal of the Kildare Archæological Society" for 1906-8, p. 452, as follows:—"In some cases the wren-boys carry round little toy birds on a decorated bier, and they themselves have ribbons and coloured pieces of cloth pinned into their clothes.

If they receive no welcome at a house, but are told to "be off out of this," there is danger of their burying one of the wrens opposite the hall-door, through which no luck would then enter for a twelve-month. Eventually at the end of the day each wren is buried with a penny."

Patrick Kennedy, in "The Banks of the Boro" (Co. Wexford) relates the following legend to account for the persecution of the wren:—

"When the Jews were in search of St. Stephen, they lost their labour for a long time, till, on passing by a clump of furze-bushes they observed a couple of wrens flying in and out, and chattering in a most unaccountable manner. They had the curiosity to pull a bush aside, and there they discovered the saint concealed. What more reasonable than to punish the poor little *drhuleen* of the nineteenth century for the crime of his ancestors committed in the first." (pp. 233-231.)

To find the origin of the custom of hunting the wren we must go back to ancient times in Ireland, when the wren was an object of superstitious veneration amongst the pagan Irish. In "Cormac's Glossary" the word *drean* i.e., wren, is explained as "draoi-en, a Druidic bird," a bird that makes a prediction, from whence is probably derived the saying, "a little bird told me," which is the great source of parents' information regarding the doings of their children, many of which the said children would prefer not to be whispered to parental ears. A bird which was an object of respect to the Druids became, almost of necessity, an object of aversion to the Christian priesthood, and the triumphant religion signalised its ascendancy by endeavouring to extirpate any object which appeared to resist it: for in striving to effect the destruction of the "king of all birds," the priests sought to deal a death-blow to the science of augury.

The hunting of the wren having been described by two such gifted Irish writers as C. J. Kickham and Gerald Griffin, it would be but presumption for the writer to use his own words, therefore here is poor Kickham's description of the hunting of the wren from "Knocknagow, or the Homes of Tipperary."

"Mat Donovan (Mat the thresher) strode up the hill with an easy swinging gait; he carried a huge stick in his hand and turned in the direction of the fort. Miss Kearney remarked that he was going to join the 'wren-boys.' "

"She should have known better than to use the word "wren-boys" in the sense she did. They are only called wren-boys who carry the wren in a holly bush decorated with ribbons on St. Stephen's Day, and many who hunt the wren do not join in this part of the proceedings. We may remark also that though the "king of all birds" is said and sung to be "caught in the furze" on St. Stephen's Day, he is invariably "caught" and often ruthlessly slain too, on Christmas Day.

"Mr. Lowe was astonished to see an excited crowd of men and boys armed with sticks, and running along either side of a thick briery fence, beating it closely, and occasionally aiming furious blows at he knew not what. After a while, however, he caught a glimpse of the tiny object of their pursuit, as escaping from a shower of blows, it flitted some ten yards along the fence and disappeared from view among the brambles. The crowd, among whom Mat the Thrasher and Wattletoes were conspicuous, rushed after and as they poked their sticks into the withered grass and beat the bushes, the poor little wren was seen creeping through the hedge, and the blows rained so thick and fast that its escape seemed miraculous. It did escape, however, and after a short flight, had just found shelter in a low sloe-bush, when Mat the Thrasher leaped forward, and with a blow that crashed through the bush as if a forest tree had fallen upon it, seemed beyond all doubt to have annihilated his kingship.

Grace, who could only see the ludicrous side of the scene, laughed till she had to catch at Mary's cloak for support, while Mary turned away with an exclamation of pain. But though she kept her head turned away to avoid seeing the little mutilated representation of the proto-martyr, even she was forced to laugh when the huge Thrasher shouted—

"I struck her! I struck her! and knocked my hat full of feathers out of her!"

"After a minute of complete silence, during which all eyes except Mary's were fixed on the sloe bush, a scream of delight from Grace caused her to look round when, lo, there was the wren safe and sound, high up in the air! Instead of taking refuge in the briery fence it changed its tactics altogether, and flew right across the field into a quarry filled with brambles, followed by all its pursuers except Mat the Thrasher, whose look of amazement as he stared with open mouth after the wren, elicited another peal of laughter from Grace, in which Mary and the young men could not help joining." (Chap. IV.)

The proceedings tending towards the capture of the wren having been described by a master hand, himself, like Carleton, one of the peasantry who when a boy had doubtless often assisted at the ceremonial, we shall now from Gerald Griffin's "Tales of the Munster Festivals," quote an account of the carrying round of the wren as described in his tale of "The Half Sir," (Chapter 1, p. 86).

"The Wren boys of Shanagolden, a small village in the south-west of Ireland, were all assembled pursuant to custom, on the green before the chapel door, on a fine frosty morning, being the twenty-sixth of December, or St. Stephen's Day—a festival yet held in much reverence in Munster, although the Catholic Church has for many years ceased to look upon it as a holiday of "obligation." Seven or eight handsome young fellows, tricked out in ribbons of the gayest colours, white waistcoats and stockings, furnished with musical instruments of various kinds—a fife, a pipolo, an old drum, a cracked fiddle, and a set of bagpipes—assumed their places in the rear of the procession, and startled the yet slumbering inhabitants of the neighbouring houses by a fearfully discordant prelude. Behind those came the Wren-boy, *par excellence*, a lad who bore in his hands a holly-bush, the leaves of which were interwoven with long streamers of red, yellow, blue and white riband; all which finery nevertheless in no way contributed to reconcile the little mottled tenant of the bower (a wren which was tied by the leg to one of the boughs) to his state of durance. After the wren-boy came a promiscuous crowd of youngsters of all ages under fifteen, composing just such a little ragged rabble as one observes attending the band of a marching regiment on its entrance into a country town, shouting, hallooing, laughing and joining in apt chorus with the droning, shrilling, squeaking and rattling of the musicians of the morn.

"After proceeding along the road for about half a mile, the little rustic procession turned aside into a decent avenue, which led to a house standing bolt upright on the top of a hillock, with a plain rough-cast front, in which were two rows of small square windows, and a hall-door with two steps leading up to it.

"Before the hall-door was a semi-circular gravel plot, in which the avenue lost itself, as a canal terminates in its basin. Around this space the procession formed, and the Wren-boy, elevating his bush, gave out the opening stave of the festive chant, in which the whole rout presently joined:—

> "To Mr. —— we've brought the wran,
> He is the best gentleman in the land;
> Put in your hand and pull out your purse,
> And give us something for the poor wran!
> The wran! the wran! the king of all birds,
> St. Stephen's Day was caught in the furze.
> Altho' he's little, his family's great—
> I pray, young landlady, you'll fill us a treat.

Chorus:
Sing, overem, overem, droleen;
Sing, overem, overem, droleen;
Sing, overem, overem, chintimicore,
Lebemegola, tambereen.

> If you fill of the small,
> It won't agree with the wren boys at all;
> But if you fill of the best,
> I hope in heaven your soul may rest.
>   Chorus as before.
>
> It is the wran, as you may see,
> 'Tis guarded in a holly tree;
> A bunch of ribands by his side,
> And the —— boys to be his guide.
>   Chorus as before.

As in Gerald Griffin's story there are only a couple of stanzas quoted, the foregoing is a Youghal version noted down by Rev. Samuel Hayman, M.A. There is a different Cork version of which two stanzas with music are quoted in "Hall's Ireland." Gerald Griffin's second quotation, which is not included in the foregoing, is as follows:—

> "Last Christmas day I turned the spit,
> I burned my finger—(I feel it yet);
> A cock-sparrow flew over the table,
> The dish began to fight with the ladle—
> The spit got up like a naked man,
> And swore he'd fight with the dripping-pan;
> The pan got up and cock'd his tail,
> And swore he'd send them all to jail."

In County Waterford while they have much the same version as in Youghal, they have the following additional verses:—

> "On Christmas day I turned the spit,
> I burned my finger, I feel it yet;
> Between my finger and my thumb,
> Sing, hubber ma dro, my droleen, etc.
>
> We were all day hunting the wren,
> We were all day hunting the wren,
> The wren so cute, and we so cunning,

> He stayed in the bush while we were a-running,
> Sing, hubber ma dro, my droleen, etc.

> When we went to cut the holly,
> All our boys were brisk and jolly;
> We cut it down all in a trice,
> Which made our wren-boys to rejoice.
> Sing, hubber ma dro, my droleen, etc.

The serenade concluded with the request, "Come, plase your Honour, ladies, ordher something out for the wran. He come a long way to see your honours this morning. Long life to you, Mister Falahee! The wran thanks you, sir," as a half-crown, flung by an elderly gentleman who made his appearance at a window, jingled on the grave walk. "And sonuher (good spouse) to you, Miss Mary, and that before the frost is off the ground. We are goin' to call on Mister Charles himself next."

"The younger of the ladies blushed deep crimson.

"Stay until Davy gives you a drink, lads," said Mr. Falahee.

"A new uproar of thanks and "long lives!" and sundry other benedictions followed the invitation, in the midst of which old Davy made his appearance at the hall-door with a tin can full of cider of his own brewage, and a smile on his wrinkled face, that showed with how much goodwill he fell into the hospitable humour of his master. The lads swarmed about him as flies do about a lump of sugar."

This is a striking and life-like description of the wren boys as enacted in County Limerick during the youth of Gerald Griffin, over one hundred years ago, when the performance was organised by grown-up young men. Later on in the century, in some parts of the country at any rate in the eighteen-fifties, it appears to have been left to boys of ten to fifteen years, but in all cases, whether men or boys carried out the performance, the money collected was spent in a jollification on the afternoon of St. Stephen's Day.

In the year 1920, Head-Constable Lyons, Fellow, sent to the Royal Society of Antiquaries of Ireland, two straw head-dresses used at a Wren-boy celebration at Newport, Co. Mayo, on St. Stephen's Day, 1919, with the following account:—

"The coronal arrangement at the top of the helmets seems intended to represent the sun. Some helmets are not so elaborate in this particular, as they have but a single loop which perhaps is intended to represent the disc of the sun. There is at least another type of head dress which is both corselet and helmet, and which terminates in a cone above the head, entirely enclosing the upper part of the body. I was unable to get one of these, as in the frenzy of the occasion all the regalia are generally destroyed before the end of the ceremonies, and in the licence of the occasion little attention is paid to a request, even when supported by backsheesh. But the wearer of this corselet-helmet dress is, I believe, called "the fool." There is also an "oinsheac" (she-fool) who is dressed with absurd and trivial gaudiness. The "oinsheac" is really a male, who acts the part of a female, and the pair during the celebrations maintain an interchange of grotesque endearments. Rude dancing is almost continuously practised by the whole gang.

"The inclusion of a male and sham female in mock conjugal union seems to imply the survival of a sexual rite, a ceremony of fructification. The straw head-dresses represent better than most simple textures the colour of the sun. The celebration is observed as a pretext to collect backsheesh, and some of the proceeds is spent in drink in the evening of the festival. The apportioning of the proceeds often affords the slight pretext needed for a row.

"Two or three generations ago the celebration was more decent and orderly, and it had not entirely lost its primitive seriousness. The whole parish zealously betook itself to hunt the wren. When one of these birds was obtained, it was placed on a gaudily decorated holly bush. Contributions were collected and expended much as at present, but with more solemnity and decency. If the processionists of two parishes met, a bloody fight was the result, as each parish fought for the honour of its own "Wran.""

The song used by the processionists is:—

> "The wran, the wran, the king of all birds—
> St. Stephen's Day he was caught in the furze.
> Although he is little, his honour is great,
> Then up, land lady, and give us a thrate.

> Dreolin, dreolin, where's your nest?
> 'Tis in the tree that I love best,
> Between a holly and ivy tree,
> Where none of the birds can meddle with me.

"A more modern barbarism adds or rather incorporates in the song:—

> Up with the kettle and down with the pan,
> A penny or tuppence to bury the wran."

"Nowadays there is no general practical celebration [in Co. Mayo]. The observance is performed by a great many small knots of small boys and rude young men, and the celebration, though tolerated, is regarded with disfavour. But the grandfathers of the present generation took the matter seriously as a vital part of the Christmas celebrations, and it was a great honour for a parish contingent to capture the "Wran" of a rival parish, and bear him in triumph with their own.

It is noteworthy that the rhymes sung by the wren-boys are and have been in English, even in places like Newport, where Irish was the prevailing speech amongst the people." Jour. R.S.A.I., 1920, pp. 61-63.

Two more accounts of this pastime may be given from modern works of fiction.

"On St. Stephen's Day the Glenmornan (Co. Donegal) boys beat the bushes and killed as many wrens as they could lay their hands on. The wren is a bad bird, for it betrayed St. Stephen to the Jews when they wanted to put him to death. The saint hid in a clump of bushes, but the wrens made such a chatter and clatter that the Jews, when passing, stopped to see what annoyed the birds, and found the saint hiding in the undergrowth. No wonder, then, that the Glenmornan people have a grudge against the wren!" Patrick MacGill: *The Children of the Dead End*, Chapter II.

The second extract is a Tipperary account:—

> "Wasn't it St. Stephen's Day?
> "The Wren, the Wren,
>   The king of all birds,

> On St. Stephen's Day was caught in the furze.
> Although he's little, his family's great.
> I pray you, good landlady, give us a thrate."

"I told Shorsha how it was that they were bringing round the Wren. He'd never heard how the little Wren had betrayed the Irish to the English one St. Stephen's Day long ago, and how every St. Stephen's Day since, the boys and men, and they dressed up, with their faces blackened or hid in comical masks, carried him through the town in the midst of a bush of holly.

> "As I was going to Killenaule,
> I met a bird upon the wall;
> I up with my stick and I gave it a fall,
> And I brought it home to the Wren-boys all."

Fearsome the Wren-boys looked, twenty or more of them, men and boys, all with blackened faces and singing:

> "Droleen, droleen, where's your nest?
> 'Tis in the tree that I love best,
> 'Tis in the holly and ivy tree,
> Where none of the birds can meddle with me!"

"Black your faces, the three of ye," says Jimmy to us." " 'Tis the one chance ye have of tricking the redcoats."

. . . 'While a cat would be licking his ear' we got back on deck and put our request to the Wren-boys to go along with them.

"Are ye 'Three-Year-Olds'?" says the leader of them. "Your sowl to glory!" says I. "'Tis 'Three-Year-Olds' the O'Mahonys always were."

When they heard that they couldn't do enough for us. . . Shouting like hearties over we went across the Causeway:

> "Holly and ivy;
> Ivy and holly!
> Christmas Day is all a folly.
> Up with the kettle, and down with the pan.
> Give us your hansel, and let us begone,
> Ub-burra-bub-burra droleen, droleen, droleen,
> Ub-burra-bub-burra . . ."

Condensed from "Travelling Men," by W. G. Dowsley, pp. 235-238.

The hunting of the wren has already been referred back to pagan Ireland and the triumph of Christianity over Druidism, but its primeval origin has its roots in much more remote past and must be referred back to the infancy of the Indo-European nations. There was a parallel custom among the boys of ancient Greece, which still survives among the youth of modern Greece. This was the "Swallow Song," an old popular song at the return of the swallows, which the Rhodian boys went about singing in the month Boedomin (latter half of September and first half of October), and afterwards begged.

> "The swallow is come!
> The swallow is come!
> O fair are the seasons, and light
> Are the days that she brings
> With her dusky wings.
> And wilt thou not dole
> From the wealth that is thine,
> The fig and the bowl of rosy wine;
> And the wheaten meal and the basket of cheese;
> And the omlet cake that is known to please
> The swallow that comes to the Rhodian land?
> Say, must we begone with an empty hand"—

CHAPTER X.

Rhymes, complimentary, humorous and sarcastic, of the counties of Derry and Antrim.

Commencing with the north, Derry rejoices in the proud title of "The Maiden City," which commemorates her two heroic sieges, the latter of which afforded Macauley material for one of the most famous passages in his history, and also inspired Charlotte Elizabeth's finest poem:—

> "A rampart wall was round her,
> The river at her feet,
> And here she sat alone, boys,
> And looking from the hill,
> Vowed a maiden on her throne, boys,
> Would be a maiden still."

Regarding which a writer says:—"A maiden city" is fit theme for rejoicing at a lady's hands. Thus our fair authoress has a double right to be a spirited chronicler of the spirited defence of that famous old maid, Derry—I hope I may say old maid without offence to a city."

The walls of Derry that did such good service in the defence of the maiden city, serve for a saying regarding any person who is very penurious and close-fisted:—"He's as hard as Derry walls," there is a variant of this saying that used to be common:—"As hard as the knockers of Newgate," referring presumably to the London prison famous in the criminal annals of bygone days.

In Derry County, Newtownlimavady, now reverted back to its ancient name of Limavady, has a very complimentary rhyme:—

> "Newtown is a pretty place,
> And stands upon the Roe;
> If you want a pretty girl,
> To Newtown you must go."

———◆———

Evidently W. M. Thackeray agreed with this from his brief visit to the town, as he devotes several pages of rhyme in "The Irish Sketch Book" (1842) to the charms of "Peg of Limavady."

> "Hebe's self I thought
>   Entered the apartment;
> As she came she smiled,
>   And the smile bewitching,
> On my word and honour,
>   Lighted all the kitchen."

Fain would we quote many more verses, not for the sake of Thackeray's poetry, but for its description for a charming Irish colleen. In the foregoing rhymes beauty appears as a principal consideration, but in a neighbouring district it is said of the fair sex:—

> "Like the girls of Munterloney,
>   You're better than you're bonnie."

A rhyme dealing with localities is:—

> "Ling, Dring and Ballyarton,
>   The three Kinculls and Bultybracken."

These are hills in sight of each other and seen from Claudy. Other rhymes of the same district are:—

> "Lettermuck, Lettermire,
>   Killaloo's all afire."

> "Aughtaugh, Ervey and Listress—
>   These three townlands are round the Ness."

> "Up in Glengarragh,
>   Where I sprung on my toe,
> The first time I sa' ye,
>   Oul' Peggy Roe."

In the southern part of the county we have:—

> "Gulladuff for lads and lasses—
>   Moyagull for goats and asses."

Another rhyme is:—

> "Upper Binn beagles, Lower Binn brocks,
> Killycor capons,[6] and Claudy game cocks."

In this couplet two words are noticeable—brock (Gaelic: *broc*, a badger), which is a common name for this animal throughout the north; and *capons*, an old English word for a table fowl, now practically obsolete.

"Banagher Sand" is proverbial for its luck-bringing qualities. The Banagher referred to is in County Derry, near Dungiven, and has the ruins of an old church, and of a small square building locally termed "the abbey." It is situated on the south side of the river Owenreagh, in a retired and beautiful valley. Both church and abbey are said to have been founded by St. O'Heney. In the cemetery there is a curious monument of St. O'Heney, and on the western side of the abbey is to be seen an effigy of the saint in a tolerable state of preservation. A view of the monument is given in "The Estate of the Diocese of Derry," by Rev. W. A. Reynell, M.A., printed in "The Ulster Journal of Archæology," Vol. II., p. 128, N.S. The earth adjacent to the monument (as in the case of St. Patrick's grave at Downpatrick), is regarded as sacred. In a horse race whoever can throw some of the Banagher sand on the rider as he passes ensures success to his horse. If a person in the locality has a lawsuit he only requires to put some of the Banagher sand in his pocket to win the case. This is so well understood that it is considered risky to go to law with a Banagher man. The sand carries virtue with it wherever it goes, but it should, to prove efficacious, be lifted and given to anyone asking for it by a genuine descendant of the Saint, and I am told that there is only one person in the district (he lives at Dungiven) who can do so at present.

Shane Crossagh, the famous county Derry robber, was buried in Banagher graveyard between the years 1725 and 1735.

Archibald M'Sparran shows the use made of "Banagher Sand" in "The Legend of M'Donnell and the Norman De Burgos," where it is used on a race-horse to prevent witchcraft or overlooking.

"He intended to go to Banagher for a little of the sacred sand to cast over the Brimmagh [a racehorse] to save him from witchcraft or the blink of an ill eye," said he. . .

"The sum of the matter was that he arrived safe at the place, entered the hallowed ground, put up a short prayer to the saint, and what was remarkable met one Murrough O'Heaney, a lineal descendant of the guardian angel of that district, and called after his name and surname. His directions were to cast three handfuls of the sand which O'Heaney lifted to him in the name of the saint over the horse as he left the stable-door in the morning, and as many over the rider, and that he might sleep on either ear in respect of witchcraft that day."

In "Irish and Other Memories," by the Duke of Stackpoole, London, 1922, the writer gives an account of "Banagher sand," in which the titled author has managed to get its virtues exactly reversed as follows:—"Peculiar powers are attributed to natural things. For instance, it is believed that if the sand at Banagher be thrown at a horse when it is running a race, the horse must fail to win; if a person, he or she for the time being becomes a liar, totally unable to speak the truth. At a trial in Derry a witness excused himself with the following remark: "I cannot tell the truth; a man who is present threw Banagher sand over me."

Just so—some graceless wag with no respect for the nobility, deliberately and with malice aforethought, pulled the ducal leg.

That the belief in Banagher sand held good towards the close of the nineteenth century, and is very likely still held by many persons in the district is shown by a case reported in the "Northern Whig," April 30th, 1894. "At Cookstown (County Tyrone) Petty Sessions on Friday, a curious superstition which is believed in by the peasantry of that part of the county, came to light. There were two parties of litigants from a mountainous district on the border of County Derry, and as they entered the court a serious disturbance took place. One of the sides alleged, and afterwards swore in evidence, that the others had thrown 'Banagher sand' at them, and on enquiry, it transpired that there exists a belief that this substance, when thrown by a man at his opponent in a lawsuit, will ensure his winning the trial. In this case, however, two on one side and one on the other were bound over to be of good behaviour, so that the virtue of the sand was only partially exercised." It seems that in order to be effective the sand must be thrown "above the breath," i.e.. higher than the thrower's nose and mouth, so as to strike or alight on the object in a downward direction.

A further case of the belief in the efficacy of sand or clay from the grave of a saint or holy person is given by Colonel Wood-Martin (*Traces of the Elder Faiths in Ireland*, II., 193). "In the abbey at Dromohaire (Creevelea), a very good priest was buried many years ago. He was such a holy man that the very clay works cures; it is sent for even from America, and the people get it from far and near. There is an iron spoon provided to lift it with, and it is generally taken away in a rag. The cure will not work until the rag, or paper in which the clay was carried away, is returned. Some years ago many old rags were to be seen at the grave, and some are still to be observed there. The grave has been filled in more than once in recent times. The country people even put the clay in water and drink it; it is put on sores as well."

The luck-bringing qualities of Banagher sand it is claimed crystalised into the proverb: "That bangs Banagher and Banagher bangs the diel." The argument in favour of Banagher, county Derry, being capable of worsting the enemy of mankind is as follows:—"In the seventeenth and eighteenth centuries, when belief in the power of the evil eye was a generally accepted article of belief, if a good horse which had not been sprinkled with this sand lost the race, he was said to have been overlooked or bewitched: but if he were sprinkled with the sand, the horse which had beaten him was said to "bang Banagher," and Banagher, or rather the horse under the protection of Banagher sand, was said to "beat the devil"; therefore, the man who owned the loser had to acknowledge that he was fairly beaten. He could not plead as an excuse that his horse had been "blinked" (overlooked), and so to this day the expression among the peasantry is "That bangs Banagher, and Banagher beats the devil."

Hotten's *Slang Dictionary* (ed. 1865) gives:—Akeybo, a slang phrase used in the following manner "He beats Akeybo, and Akeybo beats the devil." A correspondent writing in "Notes and Queries,"

22nd August, 1874, says— " 'Akeybo' is probably the name of a place, sayings of the same sort about towns, etc., not being rare. It is perhaps *Aghaboe* in Queen's County. St. Canice in the sixth century founded a monastery here for the cultivation of literature and religious discipline. So great was his reputation for learning and sanctity that a town was soon formed around it for the reception of his numerous disciples. The town has long since passed away and Aghaboe is now merely the name of the parish in which the monastery and town were situated."

There is a Yorkshire saying, the first portion of which is not uncommon in the North of Ireland:—"It beats cock-fighting, and the judges coming down to York to hang folk."

According to another explanation, Banagher in King's County, situated on the river Shannon, was, in former times, a pocket borough, sending two members to Parliament. When a member spoke of a family borough where every voter was in the employ of the lord of the soil, the reply would be "That beats Banagher." However, Co. Kerry is also a claimant for the honour. The chief of clan Carthy, who was lord over numerous other septs of his tribe, such as the Sullivans, Donoghues and Macawleys, was elected at the fort of Lisbanagher in Kerry, and possibly the pomp exhibited on the occasion was so splendid to the Irish eye as to have given rise to the proverbial sayings to the difficulty of surpassing Banagher.

Garvagh is known as "the town of the three trees." This appellation probably arose from some forgotten faction fight that was embodied in a street ballad not yet forgotten:

> "Then Captain Doey, he turned him round,
>   Till he received a mortal wound,
>   So his heels went up and his head went down,
>   At the three trees in Garvagh town."

Garvagh also finds place in another local rhyme:—

> "Kilrea for drinking tay,
>   Garvagh for asses,
>   Limavady for Irish lace,
>   And Coleraine for lasses."

We cannot pass from county Derry without recording the saying—"Your granny was Doherty, and she wore a tin pocket." The O'Dohertys were a well-known Irish clan settled in Inishowen, of whom the last chieftain was Sir Cahir O'Doherty. An explanation of this saying given recently was that in bygone times there was a great amount of illicit distillation carried on in the mountainous districts of Tyrone and Donegal. Tin pockets, it was said, were used in a certain Tyrone town by a well known smuggling family. The saying was used as a gibe or rough joke at times.

In "Dysert Diarmada," a rhyme given as current in Ulster is:—

> "The O'Doherties tall,
> From dark Donegal,
> Were the last in the field that retreated."

The important county of Antrim has many local sayings and rhymes, topographical and general, complimentary and otherwise.

Regarding the county itself we have:—

> "Antrim for men and horses,
> And County Down for bonnie lasses."

Portrush takes to itself the name of "the Irish Brighton," and of another little county Antrim coast town, a native when questioned as to his place of residence, is reported to have said:—

> "I come from Cushendall,
> Where the praties they are small,
> And they eat them, skins and all."

However, Cushendall has further claims to fame, as according to another veracious skit, St. Patrick:—

> "Built a big cathedral, the steeple five miles tall,
> Five hundred thousand years ago, in the town of Cushendall.

> "Our tarin' Dan O'Connell, sure he was a mighty man,
> The glorious Duke of Wellington was nothing to "Ould Dan,"
> The reason why his eloquence could his Saxon foes appal,
> Was because Dan's mother's cousin's aunt was born in Cushendall."

The neighbouring village of Cushendun also comes in for a touch of the rhymster's sarcasm, as:—

> "If you go to Cushendun, the stirabout is thin,
>   And they sup it out of a tin,
>   Says the Shan Van Voght."

'Tin,' by the way, means a domestic vessel similar in shape to a delph mug, made of tin plate and consequently unbreakable. Tins succeeded the wooden noggins and piggins of an earlier generation, and were in general use in farm-houses fifty or sixty years ago, to be succeeded in a large measure by delph mugs and bowls in the present day. Tins were made in various sizes from half-pint up to two quarts. The one mentioned in the rhyme would have been pint size.

Neighbouring towns have their characteristics summed up, as:—

> "Ballymoney buttermilk, Coleraine brandy,
>   Bushmills a dirty hole, Portrush the dandy."

We have also "Ballymena of the Seven Towers," which engraved on the Corporation seal does duty as the town arms—viz., the Castle of Ballymena within an orle of six towers, and the legend on the margin of the shield, "Ballymena of the Seven Towers." The term was originated by the late Lord Waveney who used to address his tenants once a year, and in one of these addresses, referring to the development of Ballymena, said, "the town had now seven towers, viz., the Castle Tower, the Episcopal Church Tower, first Ballymena Church Tower (since removed), West Church Tower, the Town Hall Tower, the Tower in the old churchyard, and the Roman Catholic Chapel Tower." This saying was seized upon by the local Press who proceeded to boom "the City of the Seven Towers," until finally the Urban Council adopted the seven towers as their official seal. There are, however, not wanting irreverent scoffers who allege that these towers consist principally of the mill chimneys that can be counted from a certain vantage point.

The adjoining district of Connor is commemorated thus:—

> "Twelve miles from the Curran (Larne), and eight from the Bann,
>   There does the great city of Condere stan'."

Connor, by local tradition, is supposed to have once been a considerable city, and a very large extent of ground, comprising the present villages of Kells and Connor, as well as a considerable space around them, is pointed out as the site of the city by those who uphold its ancient grandeur.

There is a rhyme about Islandmagee which runs:—

"Beans and buttermilk, but take it from me,
  There's nothing for nothing in Islandmagee."

It is also a saying that "there is nothing for nothing in Dublin, and very little for sixpence," so that the peninsula, can either console or congratulate itself on being bracketed with the capital.

Near Templepatrick there is a townland described as "Killygreel for potatoes and meal," and a prettily situated county Antrim village is "Doagh, where the hens go barefooted."

Adjacent to Doagh is the thriving little town of:—

"Sweet Ballyclare, where they keep no Sunday,
  And every day like an Easter Monday."

Carrickfergus, once the most important town and stronghold in Ulster, is summed up thus:—

"Carrickfergus, once a city,
  Now a wee village, what a pity."

Another rhyme is:—

"Carrick was Carrick when Belfast was a pup,
  And Carrick'll be Carrick when Belfast's busted up."

Nor has the satirist forgotten Carrick:—

"Carrickfergus is my native place,
    And I must say in praise of it,
  It merits for its ugly face,
    What everybody says of it.

"Its children rival its old men,
    In vices and avidity,
  And they reflect the babes again
    In exquisite stupidity."

"Fire Broomhedge and Megabbery's beat" is a saying relative to two townlands near the town of Lisburn. The people of the district have no explanation of the origin of the expression which may have originated in the Volunteer period, when shooting matches were common and the competition between the different companies very keen.

Belfast, in the latter part of the eighteenth century, claimed the proud title of "the Northern Athens," but with the enormous development of manufacturing industry art and literature, have more or less suffered eclipse, and the city is now more generally known as "Linenopolis," from its staple industry. It was an American visitor who observed with regard to its climate that "you would require gills to live in Belfast."

The dampness of our climate being a watery subject naturally leads up to Lough Neagh, as bordering on some of the counties already dealt with, and also of some of those to follow. Long ago at fairs the cry was common:—

> "Lough Neagh Hones! Lough Neagh Hones!
> Put in sticks and brought out stones."

This alluded to the belief formerly prevalent as to the petrifying qualities of the water of Lough Neagh, which, as is now well known, is without foundation and arose from considerable quantities of petrified wood being found from time to time in the vicinity of its shores.

In bygone times, if popular report were true, the fishermen on Lough Neagh while remaining "upward man," actually became "downward stone." Consequently they needed not, as has been facetiously said, to buy hones to sharpen their razors upon. All that they had to do was "to turn up their trousers and sharpen them upon their shins." A great convenience certainly before the era of safety razors.

The Lough Neagh fishermen's toast is:—

> "Health to men and death to fish,
> The wagging of their tails will pay for this,"

which will remind readers of Claud Halcro's toast:—". . . health to man, death to fish, and growth to the produce of the ground!" (Scott: *The Pirate*, Chap. XIII.)

The following gem regarding Lough Neagh must not be omitted:—

"Armagh (? Antrim) . . . Neare this town is a lake, called Niach, whose water has this unusual peculiarity that if one sticks a pole into the bottom, through the water, that part of the pole which touches the ground, after a few months is turned into iron; that which is in the water turns to stone; and the rest out of the water remains wood." From a German collection of wonders of the different countries of Europe, by P. L. Berckenmeyern, 1720. Note in *Journal R.S.A.I.*, 1906, p. 397.

A county Antrim rhyme for which no explanation is offered is:—

"Neil and the deil,[7] and the red cow fought,
Neil beat the deil, and the red cow laughed."

Church bells do not have it all their own way in the matter of language, as in the counties of Antrim and Down the rattling noise made by a corn-mill is supposed to resolve itself into:—

"Clitterty clatterty, late on Saturday,
Barley parritch, an' hardly that."

CHAPTER XI.

Armagh rhymes, topographical and tory hunting.

Armagh county, or rather the fruit-growing district of it, shares with County Wicklow the appellation of "the Garden of Ireland." Armagh is sometimes termed "the Marble City," from the stone used in its building and the flagging of its sidewalks. It is also generally known as "the Primatial City," from being the seat of the Primacy. It was to this office that Ottaviano del Palacio, a native of Florence, was elevated in the year 1480. The learned Italian, on seeing the condition of his cathedral city, penned a satirical Latin epigram:—

> "Civitas Armachana,
> Civitas vana,
>   Absque bonis moribus;
> Milieres nudae,
> Carnes crudae
>   Paupertas in aedibus."

Which may be translated:—

> "Armagh—'tis a pity,
> Is now a vain city,
>   Deprived of all common morality;
> The women go nude,
> The meat's taken crude,
>   And poverty there has locality."

Regarding the town and people, Ware says:—"Though Armagh by reason of its remote antiquity, its far famed schools, and its importance, was in earlier times of greater consideration than most of the Irish cities, it was, notwithstanding, not to be wondered at that, as the result of long continued ravages of war in Ulster, it was reduced at this period to shameful poverty and had well nigh come to nought."

An anonymous wag has made the following droll paraphrase of Palacio's epigram:—

> "So far from the town of Armagh being witty,
>   'Tis an extremely cocked-up and ridiculous city,
>   Man, woman and lad,
>   Their manners are bad—
>   The ladies, I wish, were a little more prude,
>   For I blush to narrate they are awfully nude;
>   If you dine with a gent your meat's underdone,
>   And your host some poor pauperly son of a gun."

The state of Armagh as described by Ware continued until well on in the eighteenth century, as Stuart in his history of Armagh, writing of the year 1748, says:—"Such of the inhabitants of Armagh who wished to purchase superfine broadcloth, or groceries of very good quality, procured them in the neighbouring village of Richhill."

It was not until the episcopate of Primate Robinson and owing to the munificence of that generous prelate, Armagh became the handsome, well-built city that we know to-day.

In the vicinity of Armagh we have:—

> "Lisnamoe for scutching tow,
>   Ballyards for blackguards,
>   Lisnadill for lying Phil,
>   Armagh for song bards."

It seems probable that the good name of Ballyards was sacrificed in the interests of the rhyme, but the reference to Armagh would be quite in order, as the popular street ballad, "Bold Phelim Brady, the bard of Armagh," was evidently in the mind of the composer of the quatrain.

The smaller towns and localities are not wanting in cognomens as "Tanderagee no pinch," a well-known phrase which when used in connection with anything means that there is no stint. Tandragee in bygone days was a famous flax market, and there was no pinch or stint in the way that whiskey was circulated when transactions in the buying and selling of flax were being arranged. Afterwards when these good old times of "fill and fetch more" had passed away, some sarcastic wight, disgruntled at the scarcity of tipple, amended the saying to "Tandragee no pinch, plenty of water and no meal." The little town has another saying and "a Tandragee way of talking" means to be always on the grumble, but what could be more friendly than when two persons meet perhaps in a distant land, and recognise each other as being from the town of "No Pinch":—"If I had known ye were from Tandragee I'd have died for ye." Then there is the well-known jingle:—

> "Armagh Town near Portadown,
>   Not far from Tandragee."

A county Armagh district bordering on Tyrone has:—

> "Killylea for drinking tea,
>   Tynan it's the dandy,
>   Cavanapole the dirty hole,
>   But Collegehall can beat them all,
>   At drinking the bottle of brandy."

Another form that is not so common is:—

> "Killyleagh's the place for tay—
>   Tynan is the dandy, oh,
>   But if you go to Middletown,
>   They'll pick your pocket handy, oh."

This rhyme has been adapted to several districts that may settle among themselves which one had the honour of giving it birth. Here are two variants:—

> "Magherafelt for buttermilk,
>   Maghera for brandy,
>   Tubbermore's a dirty place,
>   But Cookstown is a dandy."

This localised in another district becomes:

> "Lisnaskea, for drinking tea,
>   Maguiresbridge for brandy,
>   Clogher is a dirty hole,
>   But Fivemiletown's a dandy."

Further west in County Fermanagh the last line is varied to "Enniskillen is a dandy."

When any person is in a serious mood or very depressed they are said to "have a face on them as long as a Lurgan spade." The writer has been unable to find any trace of spades having ever been made at Lurgan, the town and district being devoted to the production of handkerchiefs and hand-woven damask. Several explanations have been offered, the most feasible of which is that the land of the district around Lurgan is of a rather light description and easily laboured, consequently a much longer spade could be used than in heavy clay land. Therefore a spade of this description was specially made to suit the requirements of the district in bygone days, when this implement was much more largely used in agriculture than at present, hence, when a purchaser wished for a spade of this kind they asked for "a Lurgan spade." At the time when spade husbandry was in vogue, Lurgan was known as "little England." J. Bush, in *Hibernia Curiosa*, a description of a tour in Ireland in this year, 1764, says in describing the district:—"from the similarity of its general figure, of the language, manners, and the dispositions of its inhabitants to those of the English, had for many years acquired the name of Little England; and an Englishman at Lurgan, indeed, will think himself in his own country." The handkerchief town had another appellation eighty or one hundred years ago:—"Lurgan, No Surrender!" The loyalty of Lurgan was formerly proverbial and gave rise to the once oft-repeated but now unused expression.

Another rhyme taking in a wider district is:—

> "Keady for kittens, Armagh for old cats,
>   Dungannon for pigeons, and Newry for rats,
>   Drunken Portnorris, blackguard Mowhan,
>   Cursed Markethill, starved Hamiltonsbawn."

A most uncomplimentary epithet is "Crossmaglen where there are more rogues than honest men." This is an abbreviation of what seems to have been the original form of the rhyme:—

> "Between Carrickmacross and Crossmaglen,
>   There are more rogues than honest men,"

which recalls the couplet quoted in White's "A Month in Yorkshire,"—

> "Hutton, Rudby, Entrepen,
>   Far more rogues than honest men."

The word "rogue" is used in its more ancient sense to imply a sturdy beggar or vagrant. In the old Vestry Book of Creggan, in which parish Crossmaglen is situated, there is an entry under the year 1765—

> "Resolved that £1 be given to anyone who will tell us who are the rogues who are riding our horses about the country during service."

It may have, however, a much older origin, as there is a townland in the district named Edinashara—*anglice*, a receptacle for thieves, and another townland named Annaghgad, which popular tradition makes Aonac na nGadurde—the robbers' fair. Probably the original term was Eanac-an-ngad—the marsh of the willows or osiers. See "Historical and Statistical Account of the Barony of Upper Fews in the County Armagh," 1838, by John Davidson.

Another form of the rhyme is:—

> "Did ye iver hear tell of Crossmaglen?
>   Slatternly weemin an' lazy men."

But there is another version:—

> "Did ye iver hear tell of Crossmaglen?
>   Kindly weemin an' dacint men,"

which latter version is the correct one.

However, Crossmaglen has a better title to fame than the widely known couplet, for:—

> "It wasn't the man from Shercock,
>   It wasn't the man from Ballybay,
>   But it was the daylin' man from Crossmaglen
>   Put whiskey in my tay,"

and greater hospitality in Ireland it would be impossible to show. The rhyme was made by Father Bartley, a parish priest of that locality.

In Armagh county there still lingers the couplet:—

> "Jesus of Nazareth, King of the Jews,
> Save us from Johnston of the Fews."

This was not uttered in any profane sense, but is an interesting survival of the state of society in the early part of the eighteenth century, when the country abounded with highwaymen and robbers. The person commemorated is John Johnston, better known as "Johnston of the Fews," a territory now represented by the barony of Upper Fews in the southern part of county Armagh, bordering on county Monaghan. He was a small landed proprietor, but was best known for his zeal as a Tory hunter. Unfortunately, the Irish Public Records being destroyed, it is not possible to fully trace his activities in this branch of industry, the Assize records being burned, but from the County Antrim records printed by M'Skimmin, we find him being voted various sums of money by the Grand Jury of that county between the years 1716 and 1739. According to local tradition his executioner in chief was a man named Keenan, known in Irish as "Caonan na gCeann," or "Keenan of the heads," for when a tory was proclaimed, he could be killed at sight, caught or wounded first perhaps, then beheaded, and Keenan had so many decapitations to his credit—one hundred and ten—if local tradition does not lie—that he was called "Keenan of the heads." (Preface to the Poems of Art M'Cooey XIII.)

CHAPTER XII.

Tyrone and Fermanagh Rhymes.

The Counties of Tyrone and Fermanagh are coupled in the saying:—

"Tyrone among the bushes,[8]
Fermanagh among the rushes."

Another droll saying regarding Tyrone is:—

"Sweet Tyrone you're far from home,
With barley on your broth."

"The parish of Dromore (Co. Tyrone) where they ring the pigs in the frost," i.e., they are so procrastinating that they don't ring them till the ground is frozen, when there is no need to ring them.

Dungannon prides itself on being "the town of the Volunteers," from the historic meeting of the Ulster Volunteers in the Presbyterian Meeting House of that town in 1782. Its neighbouring town is known all over Ulster as "long Cookstown." This sobriquet received a rather sarcastic addition some forty or fifty years ago according to local tradition, when a character known as "Paddy Redcoat" flourished, who habitually carried a stick decorated with red rags, hence the nickname. One frosty day as he was going through Cookstown a dog attacked him, and caught him by the leg. On stopping to pick up a stone wherewith to defend himself he found it frozen to the ground and immovable, upon which he exclaimed, "Bad luck to you, long Cookstown, where the stones are chained and the dogs loose!" However, it seems that the incident happened at an earlier time, and was merely passed on to Paddy Redcoat, as an old friend informs me that he heard the story more than sixty years ago. It was then looked upon as an ancient story, and was told of a half-witted mendicant named Raymond, who passed through the town during a severe frost. Tormented by the small boys and attacked by the dogs, his passage through the long town took him three weeks. When at length he got clear of it he looked back, shook his stick at it and cursed it as described.

This is all very well for Cookstown, but the eminent Persian poet, Sa' di, who wrote about six hundred years ago, tells the following short story in his "Gulistan" (Chap. IV., tale 10).

"A certain poet went to the chief of a gang of robbers and recited verses in his praise. The chief ordered him to be stripped of his clothes and expelled the village. The dogs attacked him in his rear, he wanted to take up some stones but they were frozen to the ground. Thus distressed he said, 'What a vile set of men are these who let loose their dogs and fasten their stones.'"

A similar anecdote is to be found in Taylor's *Wit and Mirth* (see *Shakespeare Jest Books*, edited by W. Carew Hazlitt), so that it probably reached Europe either through the Moors of Spain, the Crusaders, or merchants of the Venetian Republic who traded with the east.

In Scotland they have its counterpart in "the long town of Kircaldy." Kircaldy is in reality, as Andrew Fairservice ("Rob Roy") represented it, as long as any town in all England, with perhaps a few exceptions, but we shall no more than that honest serving man advert to its breadth.

There is another Cookstown couplet:—

"Cookstown, straight and long,
The drink's right, but the price is wrong."

"All to one side like Clogher."

This saying enjoys much more than a local celebrity and is widely known. Though the description may not be technically correct it is sufficiently apt to pass. All the business and dwelling-houses are on one side of the main—indeed the only street, while on the other side are the Protestant Hall, the Market House, the Cathedral, and the "Palace," hidden behind its gateway and long stretch of blank wall. The Bishopric of Clogher is said to have been founded by St. Patrick. There is a legend in the Clogher Valley that on one occasion St. Patrick (presumably when leaving the district) "blessed Clogher, looked at Fivemiletown, and shook his stick at Clabby." Tradition is silent as to the reason of his displeasure with the little village on the Fermanagh border.

There is another form of the saying:—"Clogher is all on one side like the handle of a jug." For its Munster equivalent see the chapter on county Cork rhymes and sayings.

An able and rather original County Tyrone clergyman of bygone days one Sunday in the course of his remarks when expounding the 122nd Psalm, used the peculiarities of the neighbouring towns to illustrate and make clear its meaning as follows:—"You see, brethren, that Jerusalem was compactly built together. It was not a long, straggling street like Cookstown; it was not like Clogher, all built on one side, with the Bishop's palace on the other; but it was a compact town like Dungannon, where every man's purloin [purlieu?] lay on his neighbour's gable."

The district has not escaped the notice of the satirist.

> "Augher, Clogher, and Fivemiletown,
>   They'd cut your throat for half-a-crown."

The one that follows is almost as bad:—

> "Dirty Augher, proud Clogher,
>   Drunken Fintona, and sporting Aughnacloy."

Another form was:—

> "Poor Augher, proud Clogher,
>   Thatched Fivemiletown, drunken Fintona."

These are merely the ebullitions of a spiteful wit, and in no way descriptive of this fertile and romantic district, with its kindly and prosperous inhabitants, to whom the author has paid fitting tribute in his history of Clogher.

The Clogher district, in addition to its interesting historical and archæological associations, has the added interest in being the scene of William Carleton's tales and stories and longer novels of Irish peasant life. In his sketch of "Rose Moan, the Irish Midwife"— by the way it was Rose who assisted in bringing William Carleton himself into the world—he gives the following account of the midwife's procedure upon her arrival at a house where her services were required:—

"Well, honey, go away now. I have some words to say afore I go in, that'll sarve us, maybe—a charm it is that has great vartue in it.

....

"Rose now went round the house in the direction from east to west, stopping for a short time at each of the windows, which she marked with the sign of the cross five times; that is to say, once at each corner and once in the middle. At each corner also of the house she signed the cross, and repeated the following words or charm:—

> The four Evangels and the four Divines,
> God bless the moon and us when it shines.
> New moon, true moon, God bless me,
> God bless this house an' this family.
> Matthew, Mark, Luke and John,
> God bless the bed that she lies on.
> God bless the manger where Christ was born,
> An' lave joy an' comfort here in the morn.
> St. Bridget an' St. Patrick, an' the holy spouse,
> Keep the fairies forever far from this house. Amen.
> Glora yea, Glora yea, Glora yea, yeelish,
> Glora n'ahir, Glora n'vac, Glora n'spirid neev.
> Amen.

. . . Having concluded them, she then entered into the house, where we leave her for a time with our best wishes."

Much might be written regarding the foregoing rhyme which appears to be a christianized relic of an elder faith, but such a disquisition is outside the scope of this work.

There used to be a favourite rhyme with schoolboys:—

> "Augher, Clogher, and Fivemiletown,
> Sixmilecross, and seven mile roun'."

There is, however, a better form of it:—

> "Augher, Clogher, and Fivemiletown,
> Sixmilecross, and seven mile roun',
> Bould Ballygawley will knock them all down."

A complimentary saying is "Full and flowing over like

Ballynahatty measure." Ballynahatty is in the vicinity of Omagh and gives the name to a Presbyterian congregation. When a person is very shrewd it is said of he or she as the case may be, that "they could keep Omagh jail."

"**Upstairs in Carnteel**" is equivalent to "nowhere," there being no two-storied houses there at the time the saying came into vogue. Carnteel was once notable as the place where a famous fair was held, but has now dwindled to a few houses. This seems to be an abbreviation of the saying regarding another Tyrone district:— "Upstairs in Orritor where they dance on the stick flure (floor)." Orritor is situated a short distance from Cookstown.

Another Tyrone appellation is "Killyman Wrackers (wreckers)," which was probably applied in the latter part of the eighteenth century to a body of "Peep of Day Boys" in that district who had been particularly active in dealing with the aggressions of the "Defenders." Plowden, in his *Historical Review*, II., 548, quotes from a speech of Grattan's in reply to "Four resolutions introduced by the Attorney General for dealing with outrages by the Defenders."

"In many instances this banditti of persecution threw down the houses of the tenantry, or what they called 'racked' the house, so that the family must fly or be buried in the grave of their own cabin." This was a partisan speech made in the course of debate, and the sentence is not quoted as a correct and impartial presentation of the facts, but as an illustration of the origin of the term.

Every Dyan man in whatever part of the world he may be, is proud to announce that he hails from "No. 1, The Dyan," this little Tyrone village being the seat of the premier lodge of the Orange Order. There is also the now obsolete term "the Dyan slashers." The use of "the" in this instance is to be noted. Moy (famous for its horse fair) is generally spoken of in the surrounding district as "the Moy," and in the Irish State Papers of Queen Elizabeth's time, Newry is always written as "The Newrie." Dyan retains its Gaelic form somewhat softened, and the definite article preceding it, although anglicised, is still used by way of emphatic distinction.

Now to conclude with a couple of county Fermanagh rhymes:—

> "Lisnaskea for drinkin' tay,
> Maguiresbridge for brandy;
> Lisbellaw's a dirty hole,
> But Enniskillen is my dandy."

Another form of it is:—

> "Lisnaskea for drinking tay,
> Maguiresbridge for brandy;
> Lisbellaw for hay and straw,
> Enniskillen it's the dandy."

A once widely sung street ballad gave the name of the "Shan Van Voght" (little old woman) as an allegorical name to Ireland. There was an extra and prohibited verse of this ditty, once very popular amongst the disaffected, which ran:—

> "Och! what will we do for linen?
>   Says the Shan Van Voght.
> Och! what will we do for linen?
>   Says the Shan Van Voght.
> Och! we'll go to Enniskillen,
> And we'll flay an Orange villin,
> And we'll wear his skin for linen,
>   Says the Shan Van Voght."

CHAPTER XIII.

Sweet County Down: its rhymes and sayings.

Downshire's noble county is known as "Sweet County Down," and the appellation has inspired a song by Rev. David Gordon, bearing the same title, to the old Irish air of "Robin Adair." Mary Banim in "Here and there through Ireland" (Part II., p. 76), writing of Downpatrick, says:—"The scene is a fair one as I saw it, bathed in the lovely summer lights, and as we entered the Convent Schools, the children were singing to the old air of 'Sweet Portaferry,' a song whose title and words are exactly descriptive of the feelings inspired by the scenery of this part of 'Sweet County Down.' The following is the first verse:—

> "Dear are thy hills to me,
>   Sweet County Down;
> Lov'd thy glens are to me,
>   Dear County Down.
> Wherever I wander,
> I grow but the fonder
> Of thy wave-like hills,
>   Sweet County Down."

It has also another claim to distinction in being the burial place of the apostle of Ireland and two others of its greatest saints.

> "In Down three saints one grave do fill,
>   Bridget, Patrick and Columbkille."

This is the rhyming translation of an ancient Latin Distich made at the time of the "discovery" of the remains, as related by Giraldus Cambrensis, who was here in that year (1185). A different English version of the distich is given in Thomas Wright's translation of "The Historical Works of Giraldus Cambrensis," (1881):—

> "Patrick, Columba, Brigit, rest in glorious Down;
>   Lie in one tomb and consecrate the town."

This is rather diffuse and not nearly so close to the Latin original as the first from Harris's "Ware," 1736.

The reputed grave of St. Patrick adjoining Downpatrick Protestant Cathedral was marked in the year 1900 with a huge natural slab of Mourne granite on which was deeply cut a suitably incised cross and lettering. Prior to this when the spot was unmarked, tourists and others were in the habit of carrying away holy earth from the grave, so much so that the sexton had to replace the earth each season to the extent of perhaps the full of a wheelbarrow.

The miraculous qualities of earth from the grave of a saint is a widespread belief, an example of which has already been given in the case of St. O'Heney, of Banagher, county Derry, and another example is "St. Senan's bed," in the island of Scattery, in the river Shannon, where according to tradition the remains of the saint lie buried. There the islanders remove the earth to scatter over their tillage, and also use small pebbles gathered from the bed in drinking water to cure disease.

Newry is known as "the Frontier Town" from its proximity to the English Pale in bygone times, and, "coming like the half of Newry" denotes precipitate haste. It has also been immortalised by Swift, who must have been familiar with the town during his long visit to Sir Arthur Acheson's at Markethill, in the bitter couplet:—

> "High Church, low steeple,
> Dirty streets and proud people."

This, however, was not the only time that "the Dane," as he was known in his day *par excellence* in Ireland, used the same idea, as it is recorded in Prior's "Life of Edmond Malone," that "Swift having preached one Sunday at St. Anne's Church, in Dublin, where there is only the basement of a tower without any spire, the building never having been finished, the present Archdeacon Mahon, who was then a boy, followed Swift when he went out of the church, and heard him grumble out:—

> 'A beggarly people!
> A church and no steeple!' "

In "A Journey to the North of Ireland in 1792," Newry Parish Church is thus described:—"The church is a very poor, ill-contrived building; and though the inhabitants have been complaining of its inconvenience for more than twenty years, it remains almost a nuisance. . . There is not in this town a public clock, nor any public lights." (*Walker's Hibernian Magazine*, 1792, p. 171.)

An English couplet having a remarkably close resemblance to the famous Newry one is: —

> "Proud Preston, poor people,
>   High church, low steeple."

Another English town having a very similar rhyme is:—

> "Chester-le-street has a bonny, bonny church,
>   With a broach [spire] upon the steeple,
>   But Chester-le-street is a dirty, dirty town,
>   And mair shame for the people."

Rathfriland is known as "the hilly town," the ascent into, and the descent out of, being so steep that it used to be a saying in the country that "your horse's wind was likely to be broken going up into Rathfriland, and his knees broken going down again."

Some rhymster hit off the position of the town as:—

> "It's a hard climb up, an' wheniver you're there,
>   You'll surely wish you'd stayed where you were."

There is, however, another and better side to the picture which should be an enticement to visitors and tourists:

> "Rathfriland upon the hill,
>   Climb to the top and you'll get your fill."

There is a very lovely song by Moore in his "Irish Melodies," beginning with "Sail on, sail on, thou fearless bark,"—set to the old air of "The Humming of the Ban"—a title which is most aptly descriptive of the heavy foaming rush of the stream from its mountain birthplace towards the lowlands, and also of the murmuring and humming sound that it makes in its course. Shakespeare has the same idea when he makes Pericles say:—

> "the belching whale
> And humming water must o'erwhelm thy corpse."
>   (Pericles, A. 3, Sc. 1, L. 64.)

There is the picturesque barony of Mourne, known far and wide as "Kin'ly Mourne, where if you ask for a drink of water they'll fry you bacon."

As an offset to this there is the term "Mourne gabbocks,"[9] whatever that may mean; at any rate it is applied in a disparaging manner to the people of Mourne by those living outside the barony. There is "Hilltown pets," applied in the same way to the people of Hilltown, and "Castlewellan, where the ducks wore the green heads." Here's a rhyme to finish the Mourne localities:—

> "Ballyray for drinking tay,
>   Brackeny for brandy,
> The Longstone—the poor man's home,
>   And the old Town is the dandy."

Holywood is known as "the town of the Maypole," claiming as it does, to have the only one in Ireland of these interesting survivals of a charming bygone custom.

In the Ards, the village of Killinchy was once known as "Killinchy in the Woods," and every bonnie County Down lass, and some in other localities as well, understands what a "Killinchy Muffler" is, and also the uses to which it can be put. For the benefit of the uninitiated it may be explained that this comfortable protection is a coat sleeve with the arm of a member of the opposite sex inside it.

The town of Ballynahinch where a battle was fought between the insurgents and the Government forces in 1798, has for its slogan, "No Pope, no pinch, no surrender in Ballynahinch."

For those who like plenty of stir and movement a suitable place of residence would be:—

> "Sweet Dromore, where they keep no Sunday,
>   And every day like an Easter Monday."

Dromore would have had its antithesis in Banbury (England), the most Puritan of Puritan towns, in which, according to a jest that obtained some circulation, men were in the habit of hanging their cats on Monday for catching mice on Sunday.

There used to be horse races held at Dromore (County Down) on Easter Monday, hence the saying. Ballyclare (County Antrim) also shares these advantages with the cathedral city. The prosperous little town has also another saying much less complimentary:—"Dirty Dromore, behind and before."

There is a district in county Down apostraphrised as:—

> "Moneyrea, honest and civil,
> One God, no divil;[10]
> Where you see them out in the fiel's on Sunday,
> Sneddin' turnips[11] the same as it was Monday."

Alluding to the Arian belief prevalent in the district and their indifference to the keeping of the Sabbath. This is pretty well matched by the neighbouring town of "Comber, where they don't love God."

There is an Ulster saying that "when a man gets his feet in lime he cannot easily get rid of it," meaning that when a man starts building he finds more and more to do. Much the same thing holds good with rhymes and sayings, many of which though localised, are to be found in widely distant parts of the three kingdoms, and sometimes with different meanings and applications.

An interesting case in point is a "Morgan Rattler,"[12] which is a name applied in the north-east of Ireland to anything super-excellent in its way, more especially in the matter of speed or swiftness, such as a horse, a yacht, or a greyhound. In the latter part of the eighteenth century there was a famous armed smuggling lugger of this name, which frequented Carlingford Lough. Captain Chesney, father of the famous General Chesney, was a revenue officer commanding the coastguards, and had charge of the coast from Cranfield to Newcastle. In General Chesney's life (p. 84) an account is given of an action between the daring crew of this celebrated boat and the revenue men under Captain Chesney. This vessel was so fast and hard to catch that anything with similar qualities was said to be a "Morgan Rattler."

In the autumn of the year 1868 there appeared an account of a conflict between two bodies of sailors in a north of England seaport. Among the weapons and instruments used in the affray, mention was made of "Morgan Rattlers," whatever they may have been. In Cornwall the word is frequently applied to a number of things that are particularly excellent or striking of their kind, what Lancashire folk would call "regular bobby-dazzlers."

CHAPTER XIV.

Rhymes of the counties of Monaghan, Cavan, Leitrim and Westmeath.

In the county of Monaghan, "**The Green Woods of Truagh**," now alas, no more, gave their name to an Irish air; there is also the saying— "The whole world and half of Truagh," which is a localised form of the Gaelic saying—"Munster a province and the half of Ireland," alluding to the division of Ireland into two halves between Conn of the Hundred Battles and Eoghan Mor, alias Mogha Nuadhat, the northern half being called "Conn's half," and the southern portion "Leath Mogha," or "Mogha's half." Another saying is "Amackalinn, where the stirabout's thin, and Tireran for the hairy butter." These are two townlands in the barony of Truagh. A rhyme already given in connection with several other counties, has its counterpart in:—

> "Ballybay for drinking tea,
>   Monaghan for brandy;
> Clownish beats them all
>   For eating sugar candy."

Clownish is the old way of pronouncing Clones by the peasantry, and is really the retention of the old Gaelic form Cluain Eois.

Castleblayney is always associated with besoms, there being an Irish air named "Castleblayney Besoms," in connection with which there are a couple of lines of an old song, probably the remains of the original words belonging to the air:—

> "Castleblayney besoms, sold in Mullacrew,
>   If I can get them two a penny, what is that to you."

Then there was:—

> "Carrickalaney where they make the stirabout cannie,
>   And Corrie for the stelk" (potatoes and beans mashed).

It was through Emyvale, a Monaghan village near the Tyrone

border, that a beggarman passed from one end to the other without receiving any alms, upon which he turned and apostrophised the place in lines that have stuck ever since.

> "Emyvale, oh Emyvale,
> If you were as free from sin as you are from male (meal),
> You would be the happy Emyvale."

According to another version he said:—

> "Then fare ye well, poor Emyvale,
> Where the stirabout's made from Indy-male (Indian meal)."

It was considered a sign of poverty to make porridge with Indian (maize) meal. This meal had been distributed gratis by charitable people, mainly Quakers, during the Irish famine, and was only used by the extremely poor. The beggarman summed up his lack of alms and the poverty of Emyvale—as he experienced it, in this striking line.

There is a little town in Co. Monaghan called Tydavnet, and in bygone days ere the advent of Poor Law Unions and Workhouses, when an inhabitant fell upon evil days and was forced to beg for a subsistence, if asked what part he came from he would reply, "Tydavnet, God help me." There is a kindred saying in the north of England. A Tickhill man when asked where he comes from, says "Tickhill, God help me." The same saying is used in several other districts of England for which various reasons are given.

I am tempted to add the instance of "Kyme, God knows," well known to all explorers of the Lincolnshire Fens.

> "It's Kyme, God knows,
> Where no corn grows,
> And very little hay;
> And if there come a wet time,
> It washes it all away."

A climatic condition of which we have frequent experience in Ireland.

In the neighbouring county in bygone times there were the "Cavan Bucks." The name "Bucks" has been applied in various ages to the *jeunesse dorée.* There is also the saying, "cute as Gallogly." Gallogly was the Governor, or Keeper of the county jail at Cavan, and once under his care there was no such thing as escaping or outwitting him. This is equivalent to the Tyrone saying regarding anyone who is very cute and knowing:—"They could keep Omagh jail."

A county Cavan townland has a rhyme very similar to that of Emyvale.

> "Ardaragh, oh Ardaragh, wicked Ardaragh,
> If you were as free from sin as you are from pratie skin,
> You would be the happy Ardaragh."

Near the Meath border there is a long strip of a village so proverbial for its little house-keeping eccentricities that it was a saying of Mullagh that "the goats were living in the bedrooms, and the pigs looking out of the parlour windows."

The adjoining county of Leitrim contains the territory of Breffney O'Rourke, anciently ruled over by the O'Rourke chieftains, whose arms are given in the following rhyme:

> "The lion rampant and the spotted cat,
> The hand and dagger next to that;
> These regal emblems doth well divine
> The O'Rourkes belong to a royal line."

According to a local legend, an O'Rourke chieftain in one of the oul' ancient wars after many days marching and fighting became separated from his followers, and being wearied, lay down to rest in an open glade. Thoroughly exhausted he soon fell asleep, and was in that condition when a spotted wild cat emerged from the woods and came purring about his face. She awakened him, and only just in time to save himself from a treacherous enemy that was stealing in upon him. This is the tradition.

As to the O'Rourkes, at all events from that day to this it is considered very unlucky for one of their name to injure or kill a cat.

In February, 1695, William Slacke, John Skerret, and Joseph Hall entered into an agreement for the erection of certain iron works in Leitrim, viz., at Dromod and Ballinamore. They were no great favourites in the country.

A quaint old rhyme hurls maledictions at all three of them—Slackes, Skerrets, and Halls, with commendable impartiality.

> "Slacke, and Skerret, and Hall,
> The d—l take them all!
> Skerret, and Hall, and Slacke,
> The d—l take the pack!
> Hall, and Slacke, and Skerret,
> The devil them ferret."

A "**Teltown Marriage**" is an expression often used in Meath in the present day. If a couple who had been married for twelve months disagreed, they returned to Teltown, to the centre of a fort styled Rathdoo, placed themselves back to back, one facing north, the other south, and walked out of the fort a divided couple, free to marry again.

This fair was established by Lughaid Lamhfhada, and was held for fifteen days beginning on Lammas Day (1st August). According to Keating, the fair was remarkable, as the inhabitants of the island brought their children there that were of a suitable age, and contracted with one another about the marriage of them.

The remains of a large earthen rath, and traces of three artificial lakes and other remains are still to be seen at Teltown. To the left of the road as you go from Kells to Donaghpatrick, there is a hollow called Lag an aonach, i.e., hollow of the fair, where, according to tradition, marriages were celebrated in pagan times.

The Teltown (Tailtean) custom of divorce for unsuitably assorted couples also obtained in Scotland, England and Wales. In Scotland the espousal was known as "handfasting." Readers of Scott will remember that in "The Monastry," Julian Avenel explains to Henry Warden his relation to Catherine of Newport:—"When we are handfasted as we term it, we are man and wife for a year and a day; that space gone by, each may choose another mate, or, at their pleasure may call the priest to marry them for life—and this we call handfasting."

A Meath rhyme that recalls the well-known Vicar of Bray runs:—

> "Who will be king I do not know,
> But I'll be Darcy of Dunmoe."

Dunmoe Castle, once the residence of the Darcys, is situated on the left bank of the Boyne, two-and-a-half miles from Navan. It is now a ruin. In the war between William of Orange and James II., Darcy is said to have entertained on two successive days King William and King James, hence the couplet.

Persons endowed with an excess of a dispose tissue are said to be "Beef to the heels like a Mullingar heifer," which, if a left-handed compliment to the individual referred to, is a direct one to the fattening qualities of the plains of Westmeath. There is also a saying:—"Going through them the way the devil went through the streets of Athlone." It is Private Terence Mulvany, as recorded by his Boswell, Rudyard Kipling ("Soldiers Three"), who describes more particularly this mode of progression.

"Mother of Hivin! but I made that horse walk, an' we came into the Colonel's compound as the devil went through Athlone—in standin' leps."

According to the best authorities, however, this mode of progression was by a hop, step, and jump, or, in country parlance, "a hap, step, an' lep." This is illustrated by the following extract from the letter of a soldier during the South African War, that appeared in a daily paper, describing the Battle of Tugela (first attempt):—

"The Boers and the Dublin Fusiliers—Just before the battle the Irish Brigade with the Boers sent a note to our Dublin Fusiliers saying that they would be glad to get an opportunity to wipe them off the face of the earth. A note was returned by the Dublins to say that they would walk through the Irish Brigade as the devil did through Athlone."

It seems that the phrase was in common use in the west of Ireland at a hurling match, or faction fight, when one particular side, or hero of it, had gone through the opposing lines with unexpected rapidity and completeness, which calls to mind the lines from Canon Sheehan's "Glenanaar":—

"Then here's to bould Casey,
Like a lion he did chase ye,
From the Galtees to the Funcheon,
From the Funcheon to the say;
Sure nayther Mars nor Hecthor
Would ever prove the victhor,
When bould young Casey's hurley,
It went dancing through the fray."

The town on the Shannon has another claim to notoriety in "**The Great Gun of Athlone**." What this mysterious piece of ordnance is, or where it is kept, the writer does not know, but in an old Orange toast the Papists were consigned to be "rammed, dammed, and crammed into the great gun of Athlone." A most unusual species of ammunition. However, that ingenious person, Mickey Free ("Charles O'Malley, the Irish Dragoon") specifies another use for this mythical weapon, in one of his inimitable songs:—

"And we still might get on without doctors,
If the'd let the ould island alone;
And purple-men, priests, and tithe proctors
Were crammed down the great gun of Athlone."

Before the Shannon was confined within proper limits, Peter's Port was the entrance for cots arriving at the southern side of Athlone. When the land became reclaimed, a man named Jack Booth acquired the ownership. Jack being a character, and also religious, erected a preaching-house at Peter's Port, from which he excluded two of his old friends with whom he had quarrelled—Billy Sproule and John Potts. Mr. Potts was then owner of *Saunders's News-Letter*, and so when the Meeting House was completed, the inscription appeared at the entrance:—

"Let not Satan's agents enter—
Will o' the Wisp, and Jacky the Printer."
                                        J.B.

He so much valued this couplet that he and his successors left it in their wills that if, at any time, their heirs permitted its removal, they should lose the property.

On which a tradesman named Jack Cuniff, noted for his cleverness and sarcasm, composed the following:—

> "The Apostle's Port would have done as well,
>   Were you but content
>   To have called it so; and few would know
>   Which of the twelve you meant.
>   St. Peter's Port this cannot be
>   While faith to Scripture's given;
>   Divines of every age agree
>   St. Peter's Port is heaven.
>   Who owns it then? It can't be miss'd
>   By those who know thy need;
>   Not Peter blest: cursed Copper Fist,
>   'Tis Judas's indeed."

"Copper Fist" was a nickname applied to Jack Booth, who was an Anabaptist.

We are told that the following couplet used to be said in the west of Ireland:—

> "Old woman, old woman, what do you want?
>   A bit of tobacco to put in my mant."

CHAPTER XV.

Galway, Kildare, and Dublin rhymes and sayings.

In the West, Galway is known as "The City of the Tribes." The appellation, "Tribes of Galway," was first applied as a term of reproach by Cromwell's forces to a number of the leading families, on account of their friendship and attachment to each other during the troublous period succeeding the rebellion of 1641, but which the latter afterwards adopted as an honourable mark of distinction. They are usually accounted as thirteen families, but if the ancient name of Deane is included there were fourteen tribes as in the following rhyme:—

> "Athy, Blake, Burke, Bodkin, Browne, Deane, Darcy, Lynch, Joyce, Kirwan, Martin, Morris, Skerett, French."

In the year 1518, amongst other regulations it was ordered that "neither O ne Mac should strut nor swagger through the streets of Gallway," and the following singular inscription was formerly to be seen over the west gate:—

> "From the ferocious O'Flaherties, good Lord, deliver us."

M. M'D. Bodkin, in his "Recollections of an Irish Judge," relates a different story of the origin of the Tribes of Galway, on the authority of Father Tom Burke, O.P. Both the judge and the great Dominican being tribesmen themselves, can afford to relate a joke at their own expense that might not be so well received by a mixed company of Galway men from an outsider. The story is as follows:—

"In the good old times a Spanish ship was wrecked off the coast of Galway. They were rescued and brought before the King of Connaught, who was a mighty monarch in those days. Solomon in all his glory was not arrayed in the least like the King of Connaught. There was, however, one serious defect in his gorgeous get-up.

Like Achilles, he was vulnerable in the heel. In plain English, the resplendent monarch went barefoot. It is not surprising, therefore, that he cast covetous eyes at the stout leather brogues in which the feet of the Spanish sailors were encased. Pair after pair—he tried them on himself in vain. The feet of the monarch were of royal proportions and the kingly toe could not be squeezed into any one of the brogues.

Thereupon, he returned the seamen to the King of Spain with handsome presents for his brother sovereign, and a request couched in the choicest language of diplomacy, that his Majesty of Spain would send in return twelve pairs of the largest brogues in his kingdom. Either the Connaught king's handwriting was illegible, or an initial letter got obliterated by the salt water. This much at least is certain, when the document came to the eyes of the King of Spain it read—'twelve pairs of the biggest rogues in Spain.' Very willingly the King complied with the strange request, the rogues were collected by proclamation and the cargo despatched. Thus were founded the tribes of Galway."

Two other Connaught counties are celebrated in the couplet:—

> "Roscommon for aitin' the mate,
> Mayo for lickin' the plate,"

referring to the rich grazing lands of Roscommon compared with the poorer soil of Mayo.

Early in the seventeenth century (1632) the assizes for county Mayo had not been held in any fixed place, although the county jail was at Cong, so that the greatest inconvenience was felt as it became necessary to convey the prisoners long distances from the court to prison. On the motion of Lord Mayo, the Crown fixed on the town (or village) of Bellcarra, near Lord Mayo's residence of Castle Bourke, as the fittest place for the next thirty-one years. After the expiration of this period, they were for half a century held at Ballinrobe and Bellcarra alternately.

Criminals condemned to death in the latter place were executed from a tree on the lands of the neighbouring Abbey of Ballintober, and hence a verse well known in Mayo:—

> "Shake hands, brother, you're a rogue, and I'm another,
>> You'll be hanged at Ballinrobe, and I'll be hanged at Ballintober."

This rhyme is known in various parts of Ireland. In Northern Ireland it runs:—

> "Shake hands, brother, you're a rogue and I'm another,
>> You stole beef and I stole bone, you'll go to jail and I'll stay at home."

"**The Nine Gores**." This saying arose from nine members of this family [Gore, of which the head was the Earl of Ross] being in the Irish parliament which met 8th October, 1751, viz., Sir Ralph, after Lord Ross, for the County of Donegal; Sir Arthur, after Earl of Arran, for the same County: Fredrick, fifth son of the Dean of Down, for Tulske; Paul Annesley, of Cottlestown, brother of Sir Arthur, for the County of Mayo; William of Woodfort, grandson of Sir Arthur, first baronet, for the County of Leitrim; Ralph Gore, of Barrowmount, for the city of Kilkenny; and of the family of Tenelick (grandsons of the first Sir Arthur), Arthur was member for the County of Longford; John, late Lord Annaly, for Jamestown; and Henry, now of Tenelick, for Killibegs. (*Commons Journal* VIII., 252-60.)

The unanimity of the nine Gores was long proverbial, consequently their influence in politics was very considerable.

The following sweeping condemnation of Irish towns was found scratched on a pane of glass in the window of the messroom at "Ould Kinsale," in the year 1839.

> "Sligo is the devil's place,
>> And Mullingar is worse,
> Longford is a shocking hole,
>> To Boyle I give my curse;
> But of all the towns I e'er was in,
>> Bad luck to 'Ould Kinsale'."

Of the Munster county that bounds Galway on the south, Ludlow, the Parliamentary General, when he entered the barony of Burrin, in the north of County Clare is said to have described it

---•◆•---

as "a country where he could find neither wood enough to hang a man, nor earth enough to bury a man in," and the description holds good of some parts of it to this day, as the bare white (limestone) rock rises everywhere, and the only vegetation consists of detached tufts of herbage growing in the crevices. Lisdoonvarna, a picturesque watering-place in the county, used to be "the Harrogate of Ireland."

We now return to the province of Leinster after our wanderings in Connaught.

"**The Pardon of Maynooth**." In the rebellion of Silken Thomas his castle of Maynooth was besieged by troops under the Lord Deputy, Sir William Skeffington. According to Stanihurst (in Holinshed), the stronghold was betrayed by the Governor, Christopher Paris, or Parese, foster-brother to Silken Thomas. After the capture of the castle, Paris presented himself before the Governor, to receive his reward. The Lord Deputy in order to more fittingly recompense him, asked him to relate what benefits he had received from his master, whereupon he, in order to magnify the service rendered, left not untold the slightest favour that he had received at his lord's hands. Sir William, upon hearing this recital, wondered how he could find in his heart to betray the castle of a lord who had been so good to him. He thereupon ordered him to be paid the sum of money promised upon the surrender of the castle, and after to chop off his head. Upon hearing this sentence pronounced Paris said, "My lord, had I wist that you would have dealt so strictly with me, your lordship should not have even this fort with so little bloodshed as you did." Among the bystanders was James Boys, former constable of Maynooth, who had resigned his office at the breaking out of the rebellion, but who may have sympathised with his old employer and who muttered "too late" in Irish, a saying which became proverbial for ineffectual repentance, so that this historical incident gave rise to two sayings:—"The pardon of Maynooth," an expression for the headsman's block or gallows, and "Too late, quoth Boys."

This story has been told of other fortresses betrayed to enemies as well as Maynooth.

The *Annals of Ulster*, A.D., 1535, give an almost similar account of the betrayal of Maynooth Castle by Christopher Parese to that given in Stanihurst, showing that O'Donovan (Vol. V., p. 1421) was quite wrong when he stated that "we may easily believe it to be one of the many pure fabrications with which Stanihurst embellished his narrative." With the slight difference in the Annals account:—"And this is the sentence passed upon him—to give it to his father, for he did not any treachery or deception, and this man that did the deceit and foul treachery on his lord, to be put to death on the plea that he would do no more of that misdeed upon them, or on someone else." (*Annals of Ulster* III., 601-3.)

Everyone is familiar with "dear, dirty Dublin," which still continues to be applied to "the car-drivingest, tea-drinkingest city in the world." The affectionate epithet of "dear, dirty Dublin" is usually ascribed to Lady Morgan, although the writer has seen it attributed to Mrs. Siddons. It is quite unlike a saying of that stately lady, and far more like a phrase uttered by the vivacious author of "The Wild Irish Girl," whose receptions in the "tea-drinkingest" of towns were the pleasantest possible. W. J. Fitzpatrick in "The Friends, Foes and Adventures of Lady Morgan," p. 119, says:—"Considering her great popularity in Ireland, it is indeed no wonder that Lady Morgan should so long have preferred "dear, dirty Dublin," as she herself called it, to a splendid house in Regent Street which the late Colburn offered her rent free."

"Tallagh talk" or "Tallagh hill talk" is a term for a braggart, or braggadocio's talk. Formerly beggars were whipped out of Dublin as far as Tallagh Hill, when there out of the jurisdiction they used to turn and abuse the mayor, aldermen and magistrates, and say what they would do to them.

There was an interesting Dublin catchword of the period, as recorded in the anonymous "Diary of Events in Ireland from 1685 to 1690," that is amongst the Ormonde MSS.

WACANCY.—June 12, 1686. "Upon the dismissal of so many soldiers, the Irish fellows that came to be listed when one asked them where they were going, they would say 'to get a wacancy,' which after proved a jeer or byword.

July 1. On the day happened a quarrel about the by-word 'wacancy' and one or two in town were killed on that account, for the Popish Officers bid the men beat any that jeered at them. Of the better sort several asked for shoulder-knots for their swords, and blue-scarlet at the shops." . . .

There is a cheery story about the once famous Judge Keogh, in connection with the use of this word.

"A number of brothers were before him, charged with killing a man at Listowel. The judge was most anxious to obtain from an important witness what share each of the accused had in the murder.

'What did John do?'

'He struck him with his stick on the head.'

'And James?'

'James hit him with his fist on the jaw.'

'And Philip?'

'Philip tried to get him down and kick him.'

'And Timothy?'

'He could do nothing, my lord, but he was just walking round searching for a vacancy.' "

Another example of the use of this word in Munster occurs in Chapter VII., of "The Collegians," by Gerald Griffin.

Myles-na-coppuleen—"was a clean a made boy as ever "walked the ground," and such a master of his weapon [cudgel] that himself and Luke Kennedy, the Killarney boatman, used to be two hours "oppozzit" one another without a single blow being received on either side. On one occasion, indeed, he was fortunate enough to "get a vacancy at Kennedy," of which he made so forcible a use that the stick which was in the hand of the latter, flew over Ross Castle into the lower lake merely from a successful tip in the elbow."

A county Dublin saying is—"He's gone to Saggart to stack blackberries," applied to those who go to a great deal of trouble for inadequate results; blackberries being the principal production of the barren hillside of Saggart and its locality. Another county Dublin epithet is a "Whitsuntide fellow." The following remark was made by a man near Merrion, on seeing a stupid fellow nearly drive his cart over an umbrella which a passenger had let fall a few minutes previously. "Oh, that's a Whitsuntide fellow, he can't eat his breakfast without breaking his plate."

A Dublin saying with a different meaning was as "Safe as Ben Burton." In a Dublin bookseller's catalogue of second-hand books issued about the middle of the nineteenth century, a broadside is thus entered—"A Hue and Cry, or Citizens' Lamentation for the Fall of Burton and Faulkner's Bank," to which is affixed the note—"Burton was considered so safe that it still exists as a word at the card tables of Dublin, 'Safe as Ben Burton.' " The erudite bookseller's explanation is only a partial one, and taken in conjunction with the broadsheet does injustice to a worthy man. Ben Burton, in conjunction with Francis Harrison, established a bank about the year 1700, and had for his clientele the wealthiest and most influential persons of the day, from the Duke of Ormonde down. The partners' wealth was reputed very great, and Burton's Bank survived with honour and credit the great panic of 1720, in which so many banks came to grief. One of the many squibs written by Dean Swift in 1725 as a help to the *Drapier's Letters*, contains a reference to these bankers:—

> "You will be my thankers,
>   I'll make you my bankers,
>   As good as Ben Burton or Fade;
>   For nothing shall pass
>   But my pretty brass,
>   And then you'll be all of a trade."

Francis Harrison died in 1725, when "Ben" took his son Samuel into partnership. Ben Burton died in 1728, while the bank still enjoyed undiminished prestige. Samuel Burton, after the death of his father, took Daniel Falkiner into partnership, which continued until 1733, when the bank came suddenly and completely to grief, after which the same expression was used sarcastically, and then to signify insecurity and instability, until "Ben" Burton became but a memory, and the proverb divested of its force ceased to be a popular expression.

The Fade (Joseph), coupled by Swift with Burton, was also a Dublin banker from 1715 till his death in 1748. Fade Street, off South Great George Street, Dublin, is named after him.

"As rich as Damer" was formerly a popular saying in Dublin

and the adjacent counties, applied to indicate a person of immense wealth. The original of the saying, Joseph Damer, was a noted banker, "money-scrivener," and usurer in Dublin. Born in 1630, he was the eldest son of John Damer, of Godmanstow, County Dorset. He became captain of a troop of horse in the Parliamentary army, and was so highly esteemed by Cromwell, that he was sent twice on diplomatic missions to Cardinal Mazarin. Not thinking it safe to reside in England after the Restoration, he sold his lands in the counties of Somerset and Dorset, and taking advantage of the cheapness of land in Ireland he came here in 1661 or 1662, and purchased large estates. His name also appears both as a grantee and purchaser of lands forfeited in the Williamite confiscations. He was conspicuous as a miser as well as a banker, and is reputed to have died worth £400,000 (an enormous sum in those days), 6th July, 1720, aged ninety.

Swift, in a skit, "The Bank thrown down," has:—

> "The ghost of old Damer, who left not his betters,
> When it heard of a bank appear'd to his debtors,
> And lent them for money the backs of his letters:
> His debtors they wonder'd to find him so frank,
> For old Nick gave the papers the mark of the bank."

CHAPTER XVI.

Rhymes and sayings of the counties of Wicklow, Wexford and Tipperary.

In the county immediately south of Dublin the Wicklow clans in bygone days were termed "The Three Scourges of the Saxons." They frequently harried the outlying suburbs of Dublin right up to the city walls; while the locality known as "the bloody fields," near Miltown, preserves the traditionary memory of 'Black Monday', 30th of March, 1299, when five hundred Dublin burgesses were massacred by these clans while pleasuring in this delightful neighbourhood, with all "their pretty chickens and their dams at one fell swoop."

The three clans were O'Byrne, O'Toole, and O'Kavanagh. Patrick Kennedy, in the "Banks of the Boro," mentions that when a child he knew "a lady who combined in her own person the blood of the three great families of Hy-Kinselach, O'Byrn, O'Toole, and O'Kavanagh, the 'The Three Terrors of the Sassanach,' as they were termed in the olden times." (pp. 172-3.)

A slightly different version is quoted in "The O'Byrnes of Wicklow."

> "O'Byrne, O'Moore, and O'Cavanagh,
>   The three would thrash the Sassenagh."

In the reign of Queen Elizabeth, Feagh MacHugh O'Byrne was a formidable and menacing neighbour to Dublin and the adjoining districts of the Pale. Thomas D'Arcy M'Gee has sufficiently described the activities of the Glenmalure chieftain:—

> "Feagh MacHugh, of the mountain—
>   Feagh MacHugh of the glen—
> Who has not heard of the Glenmalure chief
>   And the feats of his hard-riding men.
> "From Ardamine north to Kilmainham,
>   He rules like a king of few words;

And the marchmen of seven score castles
Keep watch for the sheen of his swords."

Rev. James Hughes, writing on "The Fall of Clan Kavanagh," says "another cause of its early fall and subjugation was its proximity to the seat of English power. What was said at this time of the O'Byrnes of Wicklow was also true of the Kavanaghs: "there be those who dwell within sight of the smoke of Dublin who are not subject to the laws."

An old chronicle states that the Normans landed at "the Bann (Bannow)" and remarks "that hereupon the rime runneth:—

"At the creek of Bag-an-bun
Ireland was lost and won."

The explanation of this will be found in Keating:—

"As regards Robert Fitz-Stephen he came to fulfil his engagement to MacMurrogh, and the number of troops that came with him to Ireland were thirty knights, sixty esquires and three hundred footmen, and they landed in the harbour of Banbh (Bannow) on the coast of County Wexford, at a place called Bag-an-Bun. The year of our Lord at the time was 1170, and the seventh year of Roderick O'Connor's reign."

Bagg and Bunn is probably a corruption of Bec-na-abhan, from *bec*, a common Scandinavian word signifying a promontory, and *abhan*, a river.

Shakespeare, in "King Henry V., Act 1, scene 2, has the couplet:—

"If that you France will win,
Then with Scotland first begin."

The dramatist for his historical plays used largely Holinshed's *Chronicles* (1578) and in that work it is given as "Whoso France will win, must with Scotland first begin." Shakespeare, no doubt, quoted from memory. Hall, an earlier writer, from whom probably Holinshed adapted it, has "He that will Scotland win, let him with France first begin."

The earliest reading of the modern version known to us occurs in Fynes Moryson's *Itinerary*, 1617, fol. Part II., page 3, where under

1577 he tells us . . . "but whether encouraged by the blind zeal of the ignorant Irish to popery or animated by an old prophecy:—

> "He that will England win,
> Must with Ireland first begin."

Wexford, at which this old happening took place, is "the model county," and Wexford men are all "Yellow Bellies" since the reign of Queen Elizabeth. In a hurling match which they played and won, in her presence, they wore sashes of yellow silk and the queen is said to have rapped out an oath that these "yellow bellies" were the finest fellows that had ever played before her. Their descendants would not resign the nickname for a trifle. Wexford emigrants to St. Johns, Newfoundland, have given to their "local habitation" in that city the name of "Yellow Belly Corner."

"Gorey!" shouted after a person who leaves a door open. There was an attack during the 1798 rebellion made upon Gorey by the insurgents, who carried off all the doors. A person who leaves a door open behind him is supposed to have been born in Gorey or in some other locality without doors.

In Lincolnshire they say to a person who has the habit of leaving doors open when he should shut them:—"I see you come from Bardney." In Devonshire the offender is asked, "Do you come from Topham?" In Brittany one is told:—"It is necessary to go to Paris to learn to shut doors behind one."

Another expressive Wexford saying is "the devil run to Lusk with you."

The baronies of Forth and Bargy, situated at the southern extremity of the county of Wexford, were a settlement of the first adventurers, who, in 1169, accompanied Strongbow, Fitzstephen, and Maurice Fitzgerald to Ireland, and to some of whom lands were assigned in these baronies. The result of this settlement is a dialect peculiar to the district and differing from the rest of Ireland, which colours the local rhymes and sayings.

The Forth Man's Grace after a Scanty Dinner.

"Twi baare bones upa a baare dish,
When ye Lord plaase, He may mend this,
Gin[13] we have no mo' maate it maakes mo' matter,
God save ye King, hev awaa ye platter."

Herbert F. Hore, himself a descendant of one of the old Anglo-Norman settlers, quotes from a very old alliterative rhyme, giving the characters some old Wexford families:—

"Stiff Stafford; dogged Lambert; gay Rochford; proud Devereny; laughing Chevers; obstinate Hore; cross Colfer; showy Synnot; false Furlong; gentle Brown." The county of Tipperary has many expressive local rhymes and sayings.

"Eggs and rashers for the Bansha slashers,
And the licking of the pan for the Cahir clan."

In Carrick-on-Suir there is the curious superstition that it is unlucky to buy brooms in the month of May; and the people there will not make purchases of these useful articles during the month, saying:—

"Brooms bought in May
Sweep the family away."

Then there is the saying that finds its counterpart in other localities:—

"There's nothing for nothing in Borrisokane,
Go to Nenagh and you'll get the same."

In Tipperary "a house of elegance has a slated roof, a pump in the yard, and a priest in the family."

A slightly different version prevails in county Kerry.

" 'Ah, he's a strong man,' you will hear of so and so.

'How do you prove that?' says I.

'Why, has he not his farm, and his family, with one son a priest, and one daughter in a convent, and he with a bull for his own cows.' " (S. M. Hussey: *Reminiscences of an Irish Land Agent*, p. 145.)

———◆———

"Tipperary Stone Throwers."

In "Travelling Men," by W. G. Dowsley—

"I wasn't a bad hand at firing stones myself, for if there was one thing a Tipperary lad took a pride, wasn't it that? The great game on Sundays was bowling along the country roads, and that toughened your arm muscles finely." (The last sentence seems to describe bullet throwing.)

Stones as weapons of offence were used from a very early period in Ireland. In an account of a battle fought against the Danes in the adjoining county of Limerick, about A.D. 920, and quoted in Wilde's "Catalogue," we are told "Their youths, and their champions, and their proud haughty veterans came to the front of the battle to cast their stones."

At a later date Giraldus Cambrensis, in his "Topography of Ireland," says of the Irish:—"When other weapons fail, they hurl stones against the enemy in battle, with such quickness and dexterity that they do more execution than the slingers of any other nation."

There is "Carrick, I dread you!" "When you're in Cahir you're in trouble." A play upon the word Cahir. "Rare Clonmel!" "Light of foot as a Tipperary ragman."

'Now to conclude and finish' as they say in the street ballads, here is the effort of a nameless bard on the name of the premier stone-throwing county.

Tipperary.

"There was a bard in a sad quandary
  To find a rhyme for Tipperary;
He hunted through the dictionary,
  And found no rhyme for Tipperary;
He rummaged the vocabulary,
  But still no rhyme for Tipperary;
He applied to his mother, Mary,
  To know the rhyme for Tipperary:
But she, good woman, knew her dairy.

--------•◆•--------

....

At last this bard in sad quandary,
Resolved to leave out Tipperary."

CHAPTER XVII.

Kilkenny rhymes and sayings; the Kilkenny cats.

Kilkenny has several claims to distinction. Here stood the cathedral and many another sacred fane of no small architectural beauty, hence Kilkenny was called "the Holy City," but while peace was proclaimed from its altars, war was made from its castle; for here was the seat of the Butlers, Earls of Ormond, who were at everlasting enmity with the Desmond branch of the Geraldines. It was also known as "the Marble City," whose advantages are summed up in the lines:—

> "Fire without smoke, land without bog,
>   Water without mud, air without fog,
>   And streets paved with marble."

These are literally correct—the Kilkenny coal is almost smokeless; there is great freedom from bog in the district; fogs are very unusual; and the black marble is in common use.

The earliest mention of the above lines known to the writer occurs in the *Journal of Thomas Dinely, Esq.*, giving some account of his visit to Ireland in the reign of Charles II. Anthony Sinnot also quotes it in the "Gentleman's Magazine" for January, 1801, p. 21.

The advantages of Kilkenny are admirably stated in a poem entitled "Mattheo and Honora: A Tale," composed about 1750:—

> "Of all the towns within Ierne's coasts,
>   Kilkenny justly the precedence boasts.
>   For many rare advantages which grace
>   The happy soil, peculiar to the place;
>   No smoaky vapours from her coals arise
>   To stain her houses, or obscure her skies;
>   Upon her hills no lazy fog abides,
>   Low'ring at top or flitting round the sides;

No mud was ever known to tarnish o'er
The silver bottom of her winding Nore.

....

Canice, an early saint of great renown,
Gave name to the Cathedral and the town;
A fair cathedral built with Gothic pride,
Her domes and palaces of marble made,
Her very streets with marble pebbles laid."

In Kilkenny, after the fashion of the "Tribes of Galway," there were ten noble families, mostly, as their names show, of British origin, and one, the richest and most noted of all, that of Shee, said to be of Irish extraction. Their names may be recapitulated in a couplet after the Galway fashion, thus:—

"Archdeckin, Archer, Colley (or Cowley), Langton, Ley,
Knaresborough, Lawless, Raggett, Rothe and Shee."

The Duke of Wellington is lineally descended from the Cowley family of Kilkenny.

However, lest Kilkenny should become unduly proud of its natural advantages, we have:—

"Kells was, Kilkenny is, but Callan will be
The finest city of the three."

Kells, which also gives its name to the barony of Kells, county of Kilkenny, was once of considerable importance, having a priory founded in 1183, whose prior was a lord of parliament.

There was a famous tavern in Kilkenny in the good old times, of which it was said:—

"If ever you go to Kilkenny,
        Remember 'The Hole in the Wall,'
You may there get blind drunk for a penny,
        Or tipsy for nothing at all."

But, alas for those halcyon days, they are gone, we fear, never to return.

The saying to "fight like Kilkenny cats," who, it is said, ate one another up except their tails, has also contributed its quota to render "the marble city" famous. The story goes that in the troubled times of 1798, when the Hessians quartered in Kilkenny they used to amuse themselves by tying two cats' tails together and throwing them over a line to fight. Their officer, hearing of this, ordered that there should be no more cat fights. Still, on a certain day there hung two cats on a line when the officer was heard coming, in the emergency one of the troopers drew his sword and cut them down, leaving only the tails hanging on the line. The officer on reaching the spot asked "Where are the cats?" when one of the troopers explained that they had fought so furiously that they had eaten one another except their tails. The story was too good to be suppressed, and has since helped to extend the fame of Kilkenny round the world.

John G. A. Prim, a distinguished Kilkenny antiquary, writing upon the subject in the middle of the nineteenth century, was of the opinion that the contending cats was an allegory designed to typify the utter ruin to which centuries of litigation and embroilment had reduced the rival municipal bodies of Kilkenny and Irishtown, separate Corporations existing within the limits of the city. Their struggle for precedence and to maintain their alleged rights commenced A.D. 1377, and was carried on till the end of the seventeenth century, when it may fairly be considered that they had devoured each other to the very tail, as we find their property all mortgaged and see them passing by-laws that their respective officers should be contented with the dignity of their stations, and forego all hope of salary till the suit at law with the other "pretended corporation" should be terminated.

A slightly different account of the Kilkenny cats is given in "Walker's Hibernian Magazine," 1807, p. 416. This account has been versified in a characteristic little poem which appeared in *Arlis's Pocket Magazine* for 1820.

The Marvellous Cats (Kilkenny.)

"An honest Hibernian once gazing about,
    Espied two tom cats in a fray;

> Quoth he, 'Ah, my dears, you shan't here make a rout,
>   I will soon put you out of the way.'
>
> So saying, he kicked 'em both into a pit,
>   Then closed it over with planks;
> He bid them adieu and rejoiced at his wit,
>   Which he thought put an end to their pranks.
>
> When telling this history one day to his friends,
>   They asked what he found there next day;
> If, whether the tom cats had followed their ends,
>   Or whether they both ran away.
>
> "Now, by J———," says Pat, "this I cannot endure,
>   You think that the story's untrue!
> When I went the next morning, I found to be sure,
>   Two tails—and a morsel of flue!"

About the year 1500 occurred the famous trial of Lady Alice Kyteler for witchcraft, in which she was accused of sweeping the dust of the street to the threshold of her son, muttering this charm the while:—

> "To the house of William, my son,
>   Hie all the wealth of Kilkenny town."

This was William Outlaw, regarding whom some account is given by Patrick Watters, in a paper entitled "Original Documents connected with Kilkenny," in the "Journal of the Royal Historical Association of Ireland," for 1872-3, pp. 532-3. There are a number of accounts of Lady Alice Kyteler's trial for witchcraft, the most modern and accessible being St. J. D. Seymour's "Irish Witchcraft and Demonology," published in 1913.

"Grace's Card, the Six of Hearts." At the Revolution of 1688 one of the family of Grace, of Courtstown, raised and equipped a regiment of foot and a troop of horse at his own expense, for the service of King James, whom he further assisted with money and plate, amounting, it is said, to £14,000. He was tempted with splendid promises of royal favour, to join the party of King William. A written proposal to that effect was sent to him by one of Duke

Schomberg's emissaries. Indignant at the insulting proposal, the Baron of Courtstown seized a card which was accidentally lying near him, and wrote upon it this answer: "Go, tell your master I despise his offer! Tell him that honour and conscience are dearer to a gentleman than all the wealth and titles a prince can bestow!" The card happened to be the "Six of Hearts," and to this day that card is generally known by the name of "Grace's card" in the city of Kilkenny. The ace of diamonds, for some unknown reason, is everywhere designated as "the Earl of Cork," just as the nine of diamonds is known as "the curse of Scotland."

Callan of the Wrangling. About the middle of the eighteenth century a bitter feud arose between the Flood and Agar families regarding the patronage of the borough, and the election of the Sovereign and members of parliament. Rival factions kept the town in a state of turmoil and disorder for several years, so that it acquired an unenviable notoriety for strife and litigation, and was known to outsiders by the name of **Calling a Cloumper**—Callan of the wrangling.

May you die roaring like Doran's bull.

In the small town or village of Ullard there lived a farmer named Doran, who had a famous bull, the admiration of the district. He had also a favourite dog, a great ally of the bull's; unhappily, a wandering mad dog bit Doran's dog, who bit his friend, the bull, who went raging mad. With difficulty, and not without danger, the bull was got into an outhouse, with a low thatched roof; the door was barricaded with all manner of implements, such as harrows, carts, etc. The raging animal finding himself a prisoner, became more and more violent. A daring young fellow named Devine mounted the roof of the outhouse, gun in hand, and making a hole in the thatch, reconnoitered the bull, who no sooner saw his head through the thatch than, making a spring at him, his long "crumpety" horns got caught in the beams, and he was there suspended with his hind legs on the ground. He roared savagely until despatched by a well-directed bullet from Devine's gun, and ever after the saying spread, "May you die roaring like Doran's bull."

Ullard was formerly a small town or village whose houses lined the road where not one now remains, but this portion of the thoroughfare itself is still known to local historians and antiquaries as the "street of Ullard." (*Jour. R.S.A.I.*, 1893, pp. 259-60.)

"**The priest christens his own child first.**" A poor man's wife had seven children at a birth, and as he had no means to rear them he was carrying them to the river to drown them, when he was met by an angel who assumed the appearance of a little old man, who asked him what he had in his coat. "Puppies," replied the man. "Oh," says the old man, "I want a dog, give me one." The man, after a time, had to tell the truth, when the little man said he must get them christened first. He brought him to a priest, whom he told to choose one, and send the others to six different priests, when the priest said, "Oh, I must christen my own child first." Of course the seven children became seven bishops, and when they died were buried at Treanstown, County Kilkenny. It seems a pity to disturb the legend, but in Westcote's *View of Devon*, published in 1630, the same story is to be found slightly varied to suit the locality. In it the poor man's wife has seven, and being unable to rear, is on his way to drown them, when he meets the Countess of Devon, who saves them in the regulation fashion. Westcote proceeds to quote Camerarius, who gives a similar origin to the noble race of Whelfes (Guelphs, whelps).

Rev. D. B. Mulcahy, P.P., about the year 1865, collected from a man named Molloy, a native of King's County, at that time resident in Lisburn, a variant of this legend in which St. Ciaran was one of the seven sons that were so miraculously preserved to become bishops of the church.

A more ancient version occurs in Paul Warnefred, *De Gestre's Langobardum*, lib. I, C. 15. Thus the story is thrown back to the earliest times; for the legends which Warnefred has inserted in the history belong unquestionably to the original "folk lore" of the Lombards, and have been treated so by Grimm.

"**Going out of Ireland to live in the Roer.**" This is a district of Kilkenny, in the north of the barony of Ida, not far from Ferry Mountgarrett. Consequential Wexford folk regarded it in matters of learning and politeness much as the Athenians did the Boetians in ancient times. A very similar expression is also used in many parts of Ulster to denote what one might call "the back of beyond," such as—"leave Ireland and go to the Moy," or as an old lady who had lived all her life in the vicinity of Belfast used to remark—"It's out of the world and into Holywood" (County Down).

CHAPTER XVIII.

County Limerick rhymes and sayings; Garryowen; on the nail.

Limerick is known as "The City of the broken Treaty" from the breach of the articles of Capitulation entered into between Patrick Sarsfield, Earl of Lucan, and the Lords Justices in 1691, for the surrender of the town to the forces of William III. The stone on which the treaty was signed is still to be seen on a pedestal beside Thomond bridge.

"The Treaty Stone of Limerick! the ancient city's pride,
    That oft rang loud with crash of steel, and oft with blood was
        dyed;
"Thrice holier than the treasure robb'd by England's King from
        Scone,
    Is the glory of old Limerick—the hallowed Treaty Stone!"

Limerick is also everywhere known by the more poetical name of "Garryowen," "Owen's garden," a suburb of Limerick in St. John's Parish, in which in bygone times there was a public garden, which was frequented by the younger members of the community in great numbers. The young bloods of the town were not long in discovering this place of amusement and proceeding to indulge in what they at that time considered the conduct of the young men of spirit, such as wringing the heads of all the geese and the knockers off all the hall-doors in the neighbourhood, varied occasionally by smashing the lamps or beating a watchman. The exploits of the Garryowen boys soon spread far and wide. Their fame was celebrated by some unknown minstrel of the day in that air which has since resounded in every quarter of the world, and even disputed the palm of popularity with "St. Patrick's Day."

The opening scenes of Gerald Griffin's beautiful novel, "The Collegians," are laid in Garryowen, and from this work Dion Boucicault obtained the materials for his famous drama, "The Colleen Bawn."

The tragic story of Ellen Hanly, or Scanlan, who was the original of Eily O'Connor, the heroine of "The Collegians," was also sympathetically treated by the authors in "The Poor Man's Daughter," a narrative in a serial entitled "Tales of Irish Life." There was also another account of this dramatic tragedy of real life in the "New Monthly." There is a good account in Mr. Nassan Senior's "Journals and conversations relating to Ireland." In 1868 there was published in Dublin "Ellen Hanly: or the True History of the Colleen Bawn, by one who knew her in Life and saw her in Death."

In the words of the song to the air of "Garryowen" occur the lines:—

> "'Tis there we'll drink the nut brown ale,
>   And pay the reckoning on the nail—
> No man for debt shall go to jail
>   From Garryowen a gloria."

Of "The Nail" referred to the following account is given in Lenihan's "History of limerick"—Robert Smith being Mayor in 1685, amongst other benefactions to the city also at his own cost set up in the exchange a brass table standing on a short pillar, and himself engraved this inscription on it: "Ex dono Roberti Smith majoris Limericencibus civibus." It was afterwards placed in the new Exchange, and was called "The Nail," being intended for a public place for paying down money on, though not applied to that use. It is still extant in the town hall.

This is supposed by many to be the origin of the expression, "**cash on the nail**," and "**paid on the nail**," but the explanations associating it with Limerick or Bristol are too late in point of time to be of any authority in settling the question.

An Act of Parliament of King Robert, the Bruce (Thomson's *Acta Parl. Scot.* I. 123) contains the phrase, "super unguem" for "on the nail," in the sense of "cash down." At this Parliament held at Cambuskenneth in July, 1326, the king set forth that the lands and revenues which used to appertain to his crown were so diminished.

. . .The king on his part undertook not to impose the old regal dues or to exact *priscoe* or *cariagia* except when making a progress through the kingdom, but to pay on the nail, according to the common market, for everything in the way of purveyance. The text of the Act is to be found along with a facsimile and a translation, in 'The National MSS. of Scotland,' Vol. II.

In Nashe's *Works*, 1596, we have:—"Tell me have you a minde to anie thing in the Doctor's Book! speak the word and I will help you it upon the naile." In 1600, Holland trans. Livy, "(He) paid the whole debt down right upon the naile, unto the creditor," so that the origin of the phrase still remains in obscurity.

The writer suggests the following as a reasonable explanation of the phrase. In bygone times when the coinage was badly neglected, base coin cropped up frequently in transactions between buyer and seller. When a shopkeeper detected a base coin amongst the money passing in payment or tendered by itself, he confiscated the spurious piece, and in order to effectually prevent it again getting into circulation, as well as a standing warning to others not to be trying to pass off bad money, took a hammer and nail, and nailed it to the counter where all could see it. The writer remembers in his younger days seeing coins so nailed in some of the smaller shops. Therefore in the days when base coin was common, the counters of thriving shopkeepers would literally be covered with coins thus nailed, so that a ready money customer would literally pay "cash on the nail."

Mallow has been termed "the Irish Bath." It possesses a moderately warm spring approaching in quality the hot well waters of Bristol, gushing from a limestone rock, a long assembly room, nicely laid out walks, grottos, cascades and canals, and above all fashion, drew a numerous assembly thither annually in search of health or amusement. As early as 1753 there appeared in the "Ulster Miscellany" some humorous verses in praise of the institution, of which the following lines are a specimen:—

> "For all that you are bound to do,
> Is just to gape and swallow;
> You'll find by that you'll rowl in fat
> Most gloriously in Mallow."

The verses are to the air of "Ballyspellin." Ballyspellin itself was a famous spa in County Kilkenny on which Dr. Sheridan, Swift's friend, wrote a ballad on the occasion of his visit to it in 1728. The first lines are:—

> "All you that would refine your blood,
> As pure as famed Llewellyn:
> By waters clear come every year
> To drink at Ballyspellin."

"Sherry" sent a copy of his verses to the Dean who was at that time on his lengthened visit to Sir Arthur and Lady Acheson, at Markethill, County Armagh, and Swift sent a scurrilous poem in reply, in which he roundly abuses Ballyspellin and its frequenters, and holds up for admiration the charms of the rustic beauties of Markethill. The following lines are about the best:—

> "We have a girl deserves an earl,
> She came from Enniskillen,
> So fair, so young, no such among
> The belles of Ballyspellin."

Thanks to the song composed to celebrate their exploits, all the world knows of "The Rakes of Mallow," who are recorded as:—

> "Beauing, belling, dancing, drinking,
> Breaking windows, damning, sinking,
> Ever raking, never thinking
> Like the rakes of Mallow."

> "Tallow, Mallow, Cappoquin,
> Doneraile an' Charleyville,
> Broken windows up the town,
> Hi for the Rakes of Mallow."

"As wise as the women of Mungret" is a proverbial saying in County Limerick. There was a monastic foundation and school at Mungret and once upon a time there was a deputation sent from the college at Cashel to try their skill in the languages in order to decide which was the more learned community. The Mungret scholars having fears that they might be unable to hold their own against their rivals had recourse to stratagem. A number of them dressed as women, and going to the place where the stream crossed the highway by which the visitors were to approach, they began to wash clothes. When the Cashel professors approached and asked any questions about the distance to Mungret, or the time of day, the visitors were answered in excellent Greek or Latin, which filled them with astonishment, and when they enquired how they learned the ancient languages were answered—"Oh, everyone about Mungret speaks Latin and Greek: that is nothing at all, mere crumbs from the monks' table—would you like to talk philosophy or theology with us?" This caused the strangers to hold a conference at which they determined to return home so as not to expose themselves at a place where every woman spoke Greek and Latin thus leaving the victory to "the wise women of Mungret." This story is also told of a spot adjacent to St. Molua's well, near Kilmallock. The local tradition has it that a celebrated school or college existed there, and that it was between the students of this seminary and a band of monks from Kerry, that the exchange of learned conversation took place. Canon O'Hanlon, in "Irish Local Legends," records the same incident under the heading:—"The Rival Professors, Legend of Howth, County Dublin." Gerald Griffin, in "The Collegians," tells how Lowry Looby "proceeded the hero and heroine into the cottage muttering in a low voice, a popular distitch:—

> "Joy be with you, if you never come back,
>   Dead or alive, or o' horseback."

CHAPTER XIX.

Cork; rhymes of the beautiful city and county; pleasant Bandon; Blarney.

There are a number of names for Cork city, and sayings regarding it and its inhabitants.

> "Limerick was—Dublin is—Cork will be
> The greatest city of the three."

Alluding to the military consequence of Limerick during the latter part of the seventeenth century, and to Dublin as the capital. The prophecy, for so far, has not been fulfilled whatever the future may hold.

It appears to be an English rhyme localised, and is found in "The Life and Prophecies of the celebrated Robert Nixon, the Cheshire prophet."[14] Nixon was born in the year 1467, and the rhyme referred to runs as follows:—

> "London streets shall run with blood,
> And at the last shall sink:
> So that it shall be fulfilled,
> That Lincoln was, London is, and York shall be
> The finest city of the three."

The Munster capital also rejoices in the title of "Rebel Cork," and is said to be "God's own town and the devil's own people."

Serjeant A. M. Sullivan, in "Old Ireland: Reminiscences of an Irish K.C." paraphrases this into a compliment:—"Cork's own town, and God's own people," so you takes your choice according as you belong to 'the black nort,' or the 'sunny south.'

Who, if "the beautiful city" is mentioned, does not immediately appropriate the phrase to Cork? And why? Because it was introduced as a rhyme in a ridiculous song called "I was the boy for bewitching them," which was a popular favourite about the year 1810. It ran as follows:—

---◆---

> "My father he married a Quaker,
>> My aunt she made hay with a fork,
>> My uncle's a great grand brogue maker
>>> In the beautiful city—called Cork."

The ballad has been printed by Crofton Croker in his "Popular Songs of Ireland."

"The Drisheen City"—consequent on a dish peculiar to Cork. It is not considered complimentary to a Cork man to ask him if he is a native of the "Drisheen city."

This delicacy was made from sheep's blood seasoned with pepper, salt and tansy, and was sold made up sausage fashion in the puddings of sheep.

In a song by Captain John Wood, who wrote under the signature of "Lanner de Waltram," entitled:—

Cork's own Town,

are the lines:—

> "The square has two sides, why one east and one west,
>> And convenient is the region for frolic and spree;
>> Where, salmon, drisheens and beefsteaks are cooked best,
>>> Och! Fishamble's the Aiden for you, love, and me."

It appeared in the *Cork Southern Reporter*, March, 1825.

Cork has also a similar saying to that of Clogher, County Tyrone—"All to one side like Christ Church" is a common civic proverb, applied to any extreme leader of a party. Christ Church, Cork, which was rebuilt in 1720, leans considerably, the foundation of its tower having sunk, but it is said to be perfectly secure.

Kilmallock has been termed "**the Balbeck of Ireland**" from its numerous and stately ruins. It owes its importance to the Desmond branch of the Fitzgerald family, and was first termed "the Irish Balbec" by Dr. Thomas Campbell in his "Philosophical Survey of the South of Ireland," published in 1778.

"Sketches of Kilmallock, 'the Balbec of Ireland,' " were printed in a small folio, Nov. 18, 1840, fifty copies were printed for private circulation. The volume consists of seven plates.

"**As old as Atty Hayes' goat**" is a Cork expression for venerable antiquity. It is pretty well known that this celebrated quadruped belonged to Mr. Atwell Hayes, father of the famous Sir Henry Hayes, of Vernon Mount, who was sheriff of Cork in 1790; but it is not perhaps so generally known how the exceptional age of this goat came to impress itself upon the public. It is stated by a writer to a Cork newspaper to have been in the following manner:—The animal was well stricken in years when Mr. Atwell Hayes was yet a young man. A generation afterwards, Captain Philip Allen, the son-in-law of Sir Henry Hayes, became Mayor of Cork, in 1800, and to celebrate this occasion gave a civic banquet. It happened that at the time the goat died, and Captain Allen who, like many Cork men of the period, was a practical joker, served up at the corporate board a staple dish, under the name of venison. The city fathers were in ecstacies and pronounced it prime, delicious and excellent; but not very long after it transpired that the haunch of venison considered so palatable was neither more nor less than the hind quarter of Atty Hayes' goat. (*Jour. Cork H. & A. Soc.*, 1st Ser. I. pp. 47-8.)

In County Armagh the corresponding expression is "As oul' as Killylea bog," while other phrases to express venerable antiquity are "as oul' as tay," and "as oul' as a wee hill."

Of all the towns in the county of Cork, the one that has become celebrated the world over through a rhyme attached to it is Bandon—formerly Bandon-Bridge, from the town having been founded at the great bridge over the river Bandon, Spenser's "The pleasant Bandon crowned with many a wood."

1689. In this year the town was held for King James, but the people having got timely notice that the Prince of Orange had ascended the throne, resolved not only to keep out the six companies that were being sent to reinforce the garrison, but to turn out the Jacobite soldiers that were stationed in Bandon, the signal for which was to be the ringing of the church bell at daybreak on Monday morning, which was accordingly done. It was owing to this event having taken place on a dark Monday morning that the inhabitants of Bandon have been called "**Black Mondays**," and the neighbouring peasantry still stoutly affirm that ever since a black cloud hangs over Bandon.

————•◆•————

The town is called "Southern Derry," or "the Derry of the South," from the people of Bandon having risen in the south as the people of Derry did some time previously in the north. It has the further link with the northern town that the contingent sent by Bandon to William's assistance was attached to and fought side by side with the Londonderry men at the battle of the Boyne.

In Bandon the term "Old black bull" was applied to that rigid and uncompromising religious sect, the Presbyterians. Socially an "old black bull" was as playful as a kitten and as harmless as an old horse; but he was a man of very decided religious opinions. This is a variation of the term "black mouth" applied to Presbyterians in the north of Ireland.

Dean Swift spent some time during the year 1729 in Bandon, and whilst there had ample opportunities of learning many of the characteristics of those amongst whom for the time being he lived. It is to the information thus acquired that we are indebted for the motto still so devoutly believed to be still in existence engraved over one of the gates of Bandon, although no such inscription ever existed as:—

> "A Jew, a Turk, or an Atheist
> May live in this town, but no Papist."

There is scarcely a corner of the earth that these lines have not reached and have been quoted as a specimen of the rank bigotry and intolerance supposed to prevail in Bandon in former days. It is not generally known that the original stanza contained fourteen lines as follows:—

> "A Jew, a Turk, or an Atheist
> May live in this town, but no Papist,
> He that wrote these lines did write them well,
> As the same is written on the gates of hell
> For Friar Hayes, who made his exit of late
> Of . . . some say. But no matter for that,
> He died, and if what we've heard is aright
> He came to hell's gates in a mournful plight.
> 'Who's there?' says the sentry on guard. Quoth the other,

'A wretched poor priest, sir; a Catholic brother.'
'Halt! instantly halt! avaunt! and stand clear,
We admit no such fellow, for a wretch so uncivil,
Who on earth would eat God, would in hell eat the devil.' "

In the evidence given before the "Select Committee (Session 1824) on the Disturbances in Ireland," Rev. Michael Collins, P.P., of Skibbereen, was asked:—

"Is there an inscription over the gate at Bandon now?"

"No; that is down; I do not know whether it ever was there."

"You never saw it?"

"No; nor never saw anybody that did see it." (Page 379.)

Bandon Protestantism was believed to be the *ne plus ultra* of orthodoxy and even the Roman Catholic inhabitants, whether from hearing so much about it, or being brought so much in contact with its professors, we know not, but certain it is they became absolutely tinged with it themselves, and used to institute comparisons in their own favour between them and the Protestants of neighbouring towns. "A Bandon Papist is better than a Cork or Kinsale Protestant any day" is an aphorism, the truth of which is so self-evident that it has never yet been called in question. (Bennett's *History of Bandon*).

"**Bantry Recruit.**" When in 1796 the French ships appeared outside Bantry Bay, their approach caused great alarm. The country people struck out a plan to intimidate them, and a very effective one it proved. The costumes of the fair sex in these parts comprised at that time as an indispensable essential, a scarlet cloak—the proposition was to assemble all the damsels that could be collected together, and marshal them on the heights around the bay. It was done, and the French soldiers beheld with dismay this formidable array of scarlet, the wearers whereof appeared to be "good men and true." Hence women or girls wearing scarlet cloaks were termed "Bantry recruits."

A very similar happening occurred in February, 1797, when a body of French landed on the coast of Pembrokeshire, having for their ultimate object the burning and sacking of Bristol. A force of Volunteers and Militia, besides a great number of country people, assembled with such weapons as they could muster. Misliking the state of affairs in front, and mistaking, it is said, the red cloaks of the

Welsh women for the red coats of the British infantry, the "Black Legion" surrendered at discretion without a blow.

In the **Belle Isle Expedition** the Governor, St. Croix, made use of a similar stratagem to deceive the British as to his strength. In this the French ladies of the garrison gave him valuable assistance. Clad in red uniforms they rode on horseback along the coast where they could be seen by the look-outs of the British fleet, and such was the patriotism of the French women that those who had no horses rode on cows.

Innishannon Blackbirds.

Edward Hale Adderley raised a corps of yeomanry at Innishannon. They were not exclusively Protestant as similar corps were, and as they wore a dark uniform they were nicknamed "The Blackbirds," by the "black" Protestants of Bandon, from which circumstance the men of this village are known as the *Innishannon Blackbirds*.

BLARNEY.

This now well-known and expressive word has not been treated by the compilers of the *Oxford Dictionary* with their usual thoroughness, there being no attempt made to explain how a place name came to be used as a noun to express flattery, persuasiveness, and several other things, the earliest illustrative quotation given being the year 1819, although the word must have been in use long before this as a local idiom for a cajoling tongue.

In 1602 Cormac M'Dermott MacCarthy held amongst other dependencies, the castle of Blarney. He was suspected of treasonable practices and arrested, but when asked to confess, stoutly denied them. He was then given the alternative of showing his innocence by delivering "unto the state his castle of Blarney, upon condition that if the facts whereof he was charged were not evidently proved against him the said castle should be redelivered to him or his assignees by a day appointed. At first he seemed very inclinable to the motion, but in process it was perceived that he intended nothing but juggling and devices." (*Pacata Hibernia* II., 230, ed. 1896.) The Lord President

(Sir George Carew) was both able and cunning, but the wily Cormac had no intention of putting his stronghold of Blarney in his hands if he could help it, and so kept putting it off until Blarney talk became proverbial locally.

The earliest use of the word by a literary man that the writer has come across for so far is contained in a letter from Walter Scott to his friend Erskine, dated 26th September, 1796:—"As to expressing in a preface feelings which I do not feel, apprehensions which I do not apprehend, and motives by which I am no whit moved, I hold it (so to speak) to be all Blarney, and therefore shall not indulge Mr. Mundell by any of those commonplace apologies at all." (Lord Stanford: Sir Walter Scott's *Congé*, p. 70.)

The transition of "Blarney" from a local dialect word to a recognised literary expression was in all probability due to that brilliant band of Cork men, wits, poets, and artists, that adorned the early part of the nineteenth century. Maclise, Maginn, Rev. Francis Mahony (Father Prout), Crofton Croker, and many others of more local celebrity, may have impressed the stamp of the literary mint upon what was previously merely a local verbal token.

The "Fugo Demonium" (*Bith Nuadh*, or new life), so called because it banishes demons from the persons who carry it about with them; and he who has it in his hand will have the gift of eloquence, which places it in rivalry with the Blarney Stone.

CHAPTER XX.

Rhymes and sayings of the kingdom of Kerry.

The "Kingdom of Kerry," is an alternative name for that picturesque corner of Ireland that does well to assert its claim to be called

"Queen of the Irish Counties."

Kerry was a Palatinate. The Desmond Earls were, it is well known, both proud and jealous of their Palatine privileges, and long struggled to maintain the liberties of Kerry, and the "jura regalia" of the principality independent of the royal authority.

Miss Hickson, in "Old Kerry Records," quotes from a curious old MS. history of Kerry (preserved in the Royal Irish Academy and bearing the date about 1698), the writer of which, evidently a Catholic inhabitant of the county, relates the great cruelties practised in Iveragh by Colonel Nelson and Captain Barrington who, it is alleged, hunted down the native Irish with a large bloodhound which tore and mangled them so frightfully that for generations the proverbial phrase in Iveragh describing any great misfortune or act of enmity was "**as bad as Barrington's bloodhound to us**."

An account of Captain Barrington and his bloodhound is given in Friar O'Sullivan's "Ancient History of the Kingdom of Kerry", chapter II., published in the *Journal of Cork Historical and Archæological Society*, Ser. II., Vol. V., pp. 96-97.

Kerry Dragoons. This name is given to peasants who, seated on their rough but sure-footed ponies, with a basket or creel on each side, containing a firkin of butter, gallop fearlessly down the mountain side in a manner calculated to take a stranger's breath away.

Dingle de Couch is the place where "**a man may be arrested for twopence**," but living was so cheap there that he ought not to owe the twopence. In the happy days gone by of a hundred years ago, in that favoured town, a good house was to be had for three or

---

four pounds per year. Being close to the Atlantic you could get fish for a song if you had a good voice—potatoes dog cheap, and linen for next to nothing. In the north of Ireland when an objectionable person is wished at the greatest distance that the island affords, a common saying is "**I wish you were at Dingle de Couch**," it being the most westerly town in Ireland.

The Kerry equivalent to this saying is "**As far as Tig na Vauria from Donaghadee**." The origin of this saying is given by T. Crofton Croker in his "Killarney Legends," as follows:—There was once a long time ago a poor man whose name was Donacha Dee, and he lived in a small cabin not far from a forest in the heart of county Kerry. Donacha was a very poor man and had a scolding wife, so that between his wife and his poverty he scarcely ever got a moment's peace. One day in the month of May he went out to cut firewood in the forest when he heard a voice calling him, who gave him to understand that it was St. Brendan that was speaking, and informed him that because he was a good Christian and minded his duty, he would be granted two wishes. The problem of what he would wish for so occupied his mind that night began to fall before he thought of going home, so he gathered up a great bundle of firewood, tied it well with his gad, and heaving it upon his shoulder, away home with him. Being tired with his day's work the load soon became too heavy for him, so he was obliged to throw it down. Sitting on his bundle Donacha was in a great botheration, the night was closing fast and he knew what kind of welcome he'd have if he stayed out too late or returned without a full load of firing. 'Would to heaven,' says he in his distress, 'this brosna would carry me instead of me carrying it.' Immediately the brosna began to move and carried him to his own door, while he never stopped roaring a thousand murders, he was so vexed at having thrown away one of his wishes so foolishly. His wife Vauria (Mary) was standing at the door looking out for him and ready to give him a good salleting, but she was struck dumb at the pickle Donacha was in. When she came to and Donacha had told her his story, it was then she was mad in earnest to think that he should throw away his luck. Donacha, worn out and perplexed, was not able to bear it, and at length he cried out as loud as he could, 'I wish to heaven, I wish to heaven, you old scold, that's the plague of my life, I wish to heaven that Ireland was between us.'

No sooner said than done, for he was whipped up by a whirlwind and dropped at the north-east where Donaghadee now stands, and Vauria, house and all, was carried out the same time to its most south-western spot beyond Dingle, and not far from the great Atlantic ocean. The place to this day is named Tig na Vauria, or Mary's house, and when people speak of places wide asunder, it has become a sort of proverb to say, 'as far as Tig na Vauria from Donaghadee.' A similar legend is related of Donach O'Day and his wife who were servants or retainers of Kilcrea Abbey.

Darling Nedeen. The little town of Kenmare situated at the mouth of the river of that name, was formerly called Nedeen. It once took it into its head that Lord Lansdowne, on whose property it is situated, did not patronise and encourage it as he should. Being informed that he was coming to visit it with the poet, Thomas Moore, in his company, in 1823, it endeavoured to arouse his interest by a poem which was sufficiently extraordinary to excite the attention of both the peer and the poet. The following verses serve as an example:—

Darling Nedeen.

"Oh! it's there you will see both the hedgehog and whale,
  The latter continually flapping his tail;
  Just to raise up a breeze for the fowls of the air,
  As the eagle, the jackass, or gosling so fair,
    While they sing round the cabins of darling Nedeen.

There the geese run about through the midst of the street,
Ready-roasted, inviting the people they meet
To eat, lord and squire, cobbogue and spalpeen,
From the cows they get whiskey, the ganders give milk,
An' their best woollen blankets are all made of silk.
Their purty young girls they never grow old,
And the sun never set there last winter, I'm told,
    But stay'd lighting the pipes of the boys of Nedeen."

Whether this effusion of the local muse had the desired effect on his lordship or not, Lewis (*Topographical Dictionary*) records that in 1831 "the number of houses was 170, and since that period several others have been erected in consequence of the encouragement given by the proprietor, the Marquess of Lansdowne."

The poem was written by "Lanner de Waltram" (Captain John Wood) and printed first in the *Cork Freeholder*, 30th August, 1823.

The poem appears to derive its ideas in part from the "Land of Cockaigne," a poem belonging to the latter part of the thirteenth century, wherein

> "The gees irosted on the spittle,
> Fleegh to that abbai, god it wot,
> And gredith "Gees! al hote, al hote!"

Hans Sach (1494-1576), the German poet, assures us that in Schlaraffenland the fish remain still to be caught, roast fowls, geese and pigeons fly into the mouths of those who are too idle to catch them, and cooked pigs run about with knives in their backs so that everybody may help themselves.

Kerry cows know Sunday.

"The months of July and August, when the old potatoes were exhausted, were generally months of absolute famine. Cabbages boiled in water and mixed with some milk were then the sole sustenance of the poor, who died in multitudes of diarrhoea; and a still remembered saying "Kerry cows know Sunday," recalls the time when the cattle being fattened by the summer grass underwent a weekly bleeding to make a holiday meal for their half-starving owners."

"I bless County Kerry in the distance." It is said that in consequence of the great wickedness of the people of Kerry, St. Patrick could not enter into the county to bless it, but stood on a hill overlooking that part of the country, and said "I bless County Kerry in the distance." This traditional blessing is referred to in some sarcastic verses of "Rhing Dhow," the family poet of the O'Falveys, a Kerry clan:—

> "Nasty Iveragh with the grey dragoons,
> Glencar, where the corn never enjoys autumn suns,
> Bare and rugged high mountains from that to the west,
> These are the parts St. Patrick never blessed."

Iveragh, a wild desolate district in winter, lies between Dingle Bay and the Atlantic.

N.B.—Readers will exercise prudence by seeing that they are at a safe distance before quoting St. Patrick's benediction to a Kerry man.

Another legend regarding Ireland's patron saint and Kerry is that when St. Patrick expelled the reptiles from Ireland, he only expelled the toads from County Kerry as far as the east side of the Caragh lake and river in Kerry, but not liking the country of the people to the westward, left them the toads with his blessing.

The common toad (*Bufo vulgaris*) is not found in Ireland, it is its cousin, the Natterjack (*Bufo calamita*) that is the reptile found in certain districts in Kerry.

CHAPTER XXI.

Food and boxty rhymes.

In County Antrim they have a rhyme:—

"Barley bread will do you good,
    Rye bread will do you no harm,
  Wheaten bread will sweeten your blood,
    Oaten bread will strengthen your arm."

Above may be appropriately followed by this one from Fermanagh:—

"Potatoes they are delicate food,
I know not any half so good;
You can have them boiled or roast,
Or any way you like them most."

Of all the comestibles used in farmhouse or in cottage, the one that seems to have given rise to the most rhymes was boxty.

John Davis White, in the "Journal of the Royal Historical and Archæological Association of Ireland" for 1889 (pp. 139-142) has the following rhyme and note on boxty:—

"Boxty," or "Rasp," or "Buck Cake," was made from raw potatoes grated over a vessel full of water. The starchy matter went to the bottom, and was commonly used in the making up of linen. The residuum mixed with flour and a little butter, when baked upon a griddle, made what was called "Buck Cake," or "Boxty," and was a great treat to children long ago. It is alluded to in the old lines I may quote:—

"Here is my lady come to town,
    As fine as hands and pins can make her;
  No buck potatoes shall go down,
    She must have white buns from the baker."

Mr. G. J. Hewson has added a note to this. He says he remembered when a child hearing the following rhyme repeated:—

> "What will I do for starch and blue
>> For my high call cap, and my two bow knots
> Get a 'buck,' and cut it in two, and that will do
>> For your high call cap and your two bow knots."

Bucks were a variety of potatoes. The foregoing lines refer to Tipperary and Limerick.

This may appropriately be followed by a series of boxty rhymes. The first is from South Derry.

> "Boxty on the griddle,
>> And boxty on the pan;
> The wee one in the middle
>> Is for Mary Ann."

County Armagh has the following variant:—

> "Boxty on the griddle,
>> Boxty on the pan,
> If you don't get boxty,
>> You'll never be a man."

While County Tyrone supplies its version:—

> "Boxty on the griddle,
>> Boxty on the pan;
> Three rounds of boxty
>> Is enough for any man."

The "boxty on the griddle" refers to boxty bread, a concoction of grated raw potatoes kneaded with flour that would tax the digestion of an ostrich.

The "boxty on the pan" is boxty pancakes in which equal parts of raw and cooked potatoes play a part along with other ingredients, but either article of food would afford sufficient work for the soundest digestive apparatus.

> "Two pounds of boxty baked in a pan,
> Every one came in got a farl in their han',
> Butter on the one side, gravy on the tother,
> Sure them that gave me that were better than my mother."

The following couplet hails from county Armagh:—

> "The Ballyhoy baigles (beagles) with their shins all red,
> Blowin' up the fire till the boxty bread."

This was a schoolboy rhyme and used to indicate that the boys of that locality had neither shoes nor stockings, and that boxty was all the bread that their parents could afford. The appropriate reply, in case they had not a suitably insulting rhyme to shout back, would be a volley of stones, and in the days prior to tar-macadam and steamrollers, this species of ammunition lay plentifully scattered over every road.

Here is the most characteristic of all the boxty rhymes, as well as the longest:—

> "The boxty mill began to shrill,
>   It sounded like a fiddle;
> She strained it through her ould shift tail,
>   And clapped it on the griddle.
>
> Said the mother to the daughter,
>   'I think we want some butter,
> For he seems to be a dacint man,
>   Shure we'll trate him to his supper.'
>
> So she whipped six cuts off the reel,
>   And down to Nancy Dawson;
> And the ould man in the corner cries,
>   'An' don't forget the rosin.' "

One hundred years ago when all the flax was spun by hand into linen yarn, the last verse would have required no explanation. In those days the flax, after being spun on the spinning wheel, was wound upon a reel into hanks or "cuts" of a certain number of threads. Nancy Dawson evidently had a shop and also bought yarn. The rosin that the good woman was not to forget was evidently to make "rosin sluts," which along with rushes peeled and dipped in grease, were the usual lights in cottages at that period. Tallow candles were only used on state occasions, and as for wax candles they were only to be found in the houses of the gentry. The rosin sluts were made by dipping a strip of twisted rag or other suitable wick in melted rosin, and a spluttering light they produced.

A county Cavan boxty rhyme follows:—

> "The boxty bread it took a head,
>   And travelled over the nation,
>   But when it came to —— (naming some town or locality),
>   It was there it found vexation."

The last boxty rhyme is perhaps one of the most interesting:—

> "I'll have none of your boxty,
>   Nor I'll have none of your blarney;
>   But I'll whirl the petticoat over my head,
>   And be off with my Royal Charlie."

This clearly is a Jacobite rhyme and is also interesting from the use of the word "blarney," which, if any approximate date could be assigned to the rhyme, would give a much earlier example of the use of the word than is to be found in the *Oxford Dictionary*.

The boxty rhymes may conclude with an extract from a recent novel—"Castle Conquer," by Padraic Colum, London, 1923.

"They were all in the kitchen, and Brighid began to peel and grate raw potatoes to make boxty. This gave young Michael a cue for singing a local song:—

> The Lismore girls, their eyes are red,
> Blowing the fire for the boxty-bread.

Francis Gillick watched Brighid. . . She sat with a basin before her, peeling potatoes, grating them, straining the potato-paste, mixing it with flour, and kneading it into a cake."

The following turnip rhyme, although not so famous as Dr. Johnson's, is supposed to be said by farmers of county Antrim and county Down, regarding persons who take one or two turnips out of a field to eat:—

> "You may take one, you may take two,
>   But if you take three, I'll take you."

Here is a bit of useful advice and natural history combined:—

> "The goat's a baste that kids in haste,
>   In Aprile or in May;
>   Her milk's the best I do declare
>   To put upon your tay."

It may not be amiss when recording food rhymes to give the following Ulster prescription for preserving good health:—

> "Ate your mate, an' ye'll niver be bate,
>   But quet (quit) your mate an' you're done for."

CHAPTER XXII.

Weather rhymes and sayings; moon rhymes.

A common invocation by children to Jupiter Pluvius is:—

> "Rain, rain, go to Spain,
> And never show your face again."

A County Down rhyme setting forth the merits of the various days of the week as Washing days is:—

> "Monday's wash is a dainty dame,
> Tuesday's wash is much the same;
> Wednesday's wash is next door by,
> Thursday's wash is just in time to dry;
> Friday's wash is one of need,
> Saturday's wash is a slut indeed."

In the North of Ireland the first, second, and third of April are called the "Borrowing Days." March having once begged the use of them that he might kill an old woman's cow. He was angry with the old woman or her cow, I never heard which.

> "The first day was wind and weet,
> The second day was hail and sleet;
> The third day was birley banes,
> And knocked the wee birds' nebs again the stanes."

This is a common Scottish rhyme, being given in almost the same words in Chambers, so that it came across with the Planters. There is an English variant (Staffordshire) as follows:—

> "March borrowed from April,
> April borrowed from May,
> Three days, they say;
> One rained, one snew,
> And the other day was the worst that ever blew."

However, Ireland, in addition to the borrowed rhyme, has a

story dating back to early Gaelic days. An old legend relates that the blackbird, the stone-chat, and the grey cow bid defiance to March after his days were over, and that to punish their insolence March begged from April nine of his days, three for each of his insulters, for which he repaid nine of his own; hence the first nine days of April are called the borrowing days.

> "Three days for fleecing the blackbird,
> Three days for punishment of the stone-chatter,
> And three days for the gray cow."
>
> (Translated from the Gaelic.)

The writer ventures to suggest that instead of "gray cow," it should read "gray crow," but it is given as above in Colonel Wood-Martin's "Traces of the Elder Faiths in Ireland," II., 269.

New Year was sometimes poetically reckoned from the birth of summer, the first of May, for an ancient rhyming augury says:—

> "A white lamb on my right hand,
> So will the good come to me;
> But not the little false cuckoo
> On the first day of the year."

There is another rhyme current alike in Great Britain and Ireland, respecting the cuckoo:—

> "If a cuckoo sits on a bare thorn,
> You may sell your cow and buy corn,
> But if she sits on a green bough,
> You may sell your corn and buy a cow."

The following rhyme is to be found in the counties of Down and Antrim, and it may be in other parts of Ireland as well.

Winds.

> "When the wind's from the north
> It's good for cooling broth;
> When the wind's from the south
> It blows the dust into your mouth;

> When the wind's from the east
> It's good for neither man nor beast;
> When the wind's from the west,
> Then the weather's best."

Then there is the Ulster saying:—

"East rain makes fools fain,"

on which a weather prophet remarks that 'rain with an east wind generally lasts from twelve to fourteen hours. I have always observed during its continuance a frequent breaking of the clouds and even brightening of the sky, deluding with the hope that the rain was about to cease and the sun to shine.'

In Ulster, during a snow-storm, they very expressively say:—

"They are plucking the geese in Scotland."

In Devonshire on a like occasion they say "Widdicombe folks are plucking their geese." In Devonshire dialect "Widdicombe" means the sky.

The Blacksmith's toast is:—

"Frost and rain, then frost again."

Moon Rhymes.

At the new moon it is not an uncommon practice for people to point with an iron knife at the moon and say:—

> "New moon, new moon, be true unto me,
> That I ere to-morrow my true love may see."

The knife is placed under the pillow, and strict silence is observed or the charm is of no effect. According to T. F. Thistleton-Dyer: "English Folk-Lore," the person, after pointing with the knife, invokes the Holy Trinity before saying the rhyme. In all probability the charm would be equally effective either way.

The following "Moon Rhyme," if the directions are carefully observed, will be found quite as efficacious as the previous one. A girl who desires to conjure up the apparition of her future husband must gather certain herbs by the light of the full moon of the New Year, repeating the following rhyme while she is collecting them:—

> "Moon, moon, tell unto me
> When my true love I shall see?
> What fine clothes I am to wear?
> How many children I shall bear?
> For if my love comes not to me,
> Dark and dismal my life shall be."

Then she must cut three small pieces from the sward with a black-hafted knife, tie them up in her left stocking with her right garter, place the parcel under her pillow, and whatever she dreams will come to pass.

In Galway a salutation to the new moon was, and perhaps is still, made by the person kneeling down, reciting a Pater and Ave, and then saying, "O Moon! may thou leave us safe as thou hast found us!" Another form of salutation used in Galway, which might be applied to any phase of the moon, was to make a sign of the cross, and say in an under-tone, "God and the Holy Virgin be about me!" Then follows this verse:—

> "I see the moon, and the moon sees me;
> God bless the moon, and God bless me."

Another Galway version, and a mode for females saluting the new moon, is tripping to the nearest stile, or gate, and looking over it thrice. The person then looks up to the moon and exclaims:—

> "All hail to thee, Moon! all hail to thee!
> I prithee, good moon, reveal to me
> This night, who my husband shall be."

Great honour used to be paid to the full moon; it was the witching time for young girls to pry into futurity, with a hope of obtaining in their dreams, a sight of the husband in store for them. The invocation used at this period, as related by a Kildare woman, runs in this form:—

> "Good morrow, Full Moon!
>   Good morrow to thee!
> Tell me ere this time to-morrow,
>   Who my true love shall be—
>   The colour of his hair,
>   The clothes that he shall wear,
> And the day he'll be married to me."
>   O'Hanlon: *Irish Folk-Lore*, 191-2.

In county Derry they have a weather rhyme that is a variant of the current English one:—

> "The farmer in May
>   Comes weeping away—
>   He goes back in June
>   And changes his tune."

The meaning of which is that May in the north of Ireland is generally a cold month in which there is very little growth of vegetation, while in June, refreshed by warmer showers, it begins to spring up.

In the baronies of Forth, and Bargy (Co. Wexford) there is an old saying that:—

> "When Carrick-a-Dee wears a hat [a cloud],
>   Let Forth and Bargy beware of that."

Forth mountain is a rugged elevation extending from within three miles of the town of Wexford, about the same distance in a south-westerly direction, with a mean width of two miles. It is conspicuous by its rocky and splintered pinnacles, which rise into a variety of fantastic forms, and command a grand and very extensive prospect. The principal of these are named Carrick-a-Shinna, Carrick-a-Dee, Carrick-a-Foyle.

Owing to its variability a perennial subject of conversation in Ireland is the weather. During Queen Victoria's reign the fine weather prevailing on the occasion of Royal visits became proverbial, but we find at a much earlier date in Ireland a similar expression applied to semi-royalty, in "Butler's weather," which is explained on the following extract from a letter of Lemuel Kingdom, to the Earl of Arran, Lord Deputy to the Lord Lieutenant, the Duke of Ormonde, under date of 27th April, 1683. . .

"The miles hitherto, as your Excellency forewarned me, are very short, and the ways very good indeed; the weather is such that I believe I am a by-blow of your family, for it has been **Butler's weather** every hour since I left you." Against this the braying of asses is said to portend rain, hence the Rutlandshire couplet:—

> "Hark! I hear the asses bray,
> We shall have some rain to-day."

In Suffolk, however, when an ass brays, the usual remark is— "Another good Irishman's dead." In some parts of Derbyshire where the manufacture of hosiery is carried on, the saying is "Another stockinger dead."

In "The Zoologist," for March, 1867, is a paper by Mr. Harry Blake-Knox, wherein the following lines are quoted. He says: —"I quite believe the popular opinion that the gull seeks the land during stormy weather more than during fine weather, and on such occasions flies much further inland.

> "Seagull, seagull, sit on the strand,
> God help the poor sailors when they come to land."

Carrickfergus fishermen, if a figure appears in the morning in the clouds like part of a rainbow, which they call a Dog, expect stormy weather; if it is seen in the evening, the reverse; hence the adage:—

> "A dog at night is the sailors' delight,
> A dog in the morning will bark before night."

By some the appearance is called a "weather-gaw." If a star is seen near the moon, which they call **Hurlbassey**, tempestuous weather is looked for by them." M'Skimin: *History of Carrickfergus*, 3rd ed., p. 272.

In Cork and Kerry, at the other end of the island, they have an altogether different rhyme in which the barometer figures instead of natural phenomena.

———•◆•———

"When the glass is high, oh, very,
  There'll be rain in Cork and Kerry;
  When the glass is low of lork,
  There'll be rain in Kerry and Cork."

This seems "Hobson's Choice" of weather.

CHAPTER XXIII.

Medical charms; lovers' charms; advice to bachelors; plant lore.

A suitable rhyme would seem to be almost a necessary adjunct to the effective working of a charm, whether it be for the cure of cramp, or, for a girl, the vision of her future husband. Having mentioned cramp, the following rhyme may prove useful in alleviating that distressing ailment:—

> "The devil is tying a knot in my leg,
> Mark, Luke, and John, unloose it, I beg;
> Crosses three are made to ease you,
> Two for the thieves and one for the blessed Jesu."

Apparently the author of the verse had a poor opinion of the medical skill of the Evangelist Matthew, while the two thieves receive prominent notice.

Vervain Rhyme.

A plant that figures in folk-lore is "Verbena Officinalis," or Vervain. It is esteemed in many cases a sovereign remedy. When the plant is being pulled from the ground the following incantation is used:—

> "Vervain, thou growest upon holy ground,
> On Mount Calvary thou wert found,
> Thou curest all sores, and all diseases,
> And in the name of the Holy Jesus,
> I pull you out of the ground."

The superstition of the ancient cult is here transferred to the present professed religion, for the ground work of the charm has apparently been retained, but the words of Christian ritual substituted for the ancient deities of the land.

Penitory Rhyme.

According to T. F. Thistleton-Dyer: "Folk-lore of Plants," *Parietaria Officinalis* is known as "peniterry," and is thus described in "Father Connell," by the O'Hara Family (Chap. XII.):—

"A weed called, locally at least, peniterry, to which the suddenly terrified (schoolboy) idler might run in his need, and having grasped it hard and threateningly and repeating the following words of power:—

> "Peniterry, peniterry, that grows by the wall,
> Save me from whipping, or I'll pull you, roots and all."

Butter Charm.

In bygone days belief in the evil eye and in the power of overlooking was general, and still obtains in remote districts. Witches, it was also believed, could, by means of their unhallowed arts, take to themselves the butter of neighbour farmers. A charm against this is directly after sunset, to bar every door and window in the house, light a great fire of turf on the hearth, and place nine irons in the fire, while the following charm is recited in Irish:—

> Come, butter, come,
> Come, butter, come,
> Peter stands at the gate,
> Waiting for a buttered cake.
> Come, butter, come.

As the irons become heated a great noise will be heard without, and the witch trying to force an entrance, beseeching the inmates of the house to take the irons off the fire as they are burning her. Finding all attempts at entry useless, the witch shrieking with agony, will return to her house and bring back all the butter. The irons may then be taken from the fire, her torments will cease, and the farmer will enjoy in undiminished quantity, the product of his cows.

First of May.—Formerly every district, almost every village, had some sibylline-like dealer in charms—some old hag, who half believed in the credulity she excited. Children were brought to her to bathe their eyes with concoctions, and to fasten slips of witch-hazel round their necks, so that the evil eye could not rest on them. Maidens purchased the dew she gathered on a May morning in preference to any they could collect themselves.

> "The fair maid who, the first of May,
> Goes to the field at break of day,
> And washes in dew from the hawthorn tree,
> Will ever after handsome be."

The Greeks use the blade bone of a lamb, held up against the light as a means of foretelling future events, and in Ireland the peasant girls seek on the hill-side and in the fields for the weather-bleached blade-bone of a sheep, which is kept till the moon is at the full, and stabbed with a knife at mid-night, while the following conjuration repeated is potent to recall the affection of a wavering or neglectful lover:—

> "It is not this bone I mean to stick,
> But my true love's heart I mean to prick;
> Wishing him neither rest nor sleep,
> Until with me he comes to speak."

If by any means the bone can be placed under the pillow of the lover, the charm will be more efficacious.

Yarrow Rhyme.

Instead of the foregoing some girls gather milfoil, or yarrow, upon May, and All Hallows' Eves, place the plant under their pillows, and so dream of their future husbands. The herb also banishes evil spirits from those who carry it about their person, and if placed inside the shoe, beneath the foot, endows them with temporary fluency of speech. Yarrow is called in the Gaelic, "the herb of seven cures," from its many virtues. Girls dance round it and sing:—

> "Yarrow, yarrow, yarrow,
> I bid you good morrow,
> And tell me before to-morrow
> Who my true love shall be."

The Nine Keys.

Get nine small keys—they must be all your own—by begging or purchase (borrowing will not do, nor must you tell what you want them for); plait a three-plaited band of your own hair, and tie them together, fastening the ends with nine knots; fasten them with one of your garters to your left wrist on going to bed, and bind the other garter round your head; and say:—

> St. Peter, take it not amiss,
> To try your favour I've done this;
> You are the ruler of the keys,
> Favour me, then, if you please;
> Let me, then, your influence prove,
> And see my dear and wedded love.

This must be done on the eve of St. Peter's, and is an old charm said to have been used by the maidens in Rome who put great faith in it.

To turn to the more innocent felicities of rural life, the writer remembers his father on the "harvest rig" taking a blue flower that grew amongst the corn, and while holding it betwixt his fingers, saying:—

> "Curl-daddy grows in the meadow,
> Turn round when I bid you."

The flower turned round obedient to command, but we children were sceptical, and suspected some manipulation. This was in County Tyrone, but W. H. Patterson, in a "Glossary of Antrim and Down Dialect," says children twist the stalk of this flower (the blue scabious—*scabiosa succisa*), and as it slowly untwists in the hand, say to it:—

> "Curly doddy, on the midden,
> Turn roun' an' do my biddin'."

In Scotland (Fifeshire) the plant is called Curl Doddy, and the children thus address it:—

> "Curl doddy, do my biddin',
> Soop[15] my house and shool[16] my middin'[17]."

Another little rustic rhyme that is used for prognosticating the future is "Even ash." This is the mode of procedure in the counties of Antrim and Down. An ash leaf with an even number of leaflets is used in a kind of divination. The young girl who finds one repeats the words:—

> "This even ash I hold in my han',
> The first I meet is my true man."

She then asks the first male person she meets what his Christian name is, and this will be the name of her future husband.

Another harmless mode of divination is by the finger nails. The little white marks that come and go on the nails are subject to the following divining rhyme. We begin at the thumb:—

> "A gift, a friend, a foe,
> A lover, a journey to go."

There is also another finger nail rhyme:—

> "A gift on the thumb will surely come,
> A gift on the finger will surely linger."

Fortune telling and herbal remedies are often associated, especially in the hands of spaewives and others of that class, and the following, if it does no good, cannot do any great harm:—

> "Robin-run-the-hedge for hives,
> Rose-noble for the ague;
> Tormenting root drink all your lives
> To banish ills that plague you."

As the writer saw Robin-run-the-hedge (*Galium aparine*) used fifty years ago, the juice was extracted and boiled with sugar; in this form it was used as a remedy for hives on children. Some used the juice mixed with whiskey. This was probably for grown-ups. Rose-noble is the knotted fig-wort, and tormenting root, Tormentil.

Here is a very comforting saying for lovers:—"Kissing is out of season when the whin[18] is out of bloom."

Not so pleasant for boys and girls is the saying that on Michaelmas Day (September 29th), the devil puts his foot on the blackberries.

Another form is that the "old gentleman" puts his club on them, thus making them unwholesome. This belief is by no means peculiar to the Emerald Isle, being prevalent in the south of England, especially in Somerset, Devon and Sussex. An English clergyman tells of a boy who stated that he actually saw the devil's club come hurtling over a dyke among the brambles. Needless to say, his enjoyment of blackberries was over for that season. The writer does not know whether the worthy cleric belonged to the new or old school of theology. This belief is not so common in the north of England, though Henderson, in his "Folk-lore of the Northern Counties," says that it occurs on the Tweed side.

Now to conclude with some of the wise sayings of Mrs. Twiggelty in "Chronicles of the Coort" (Belfast).

Sez Sally Ann, "When your right han's itchy yer gonna git a strange shakehauns."

"Ay, an' when yer left haun's itchy yer gonna get money," ses Teeshie.

"A wish to goodness mine was itchy now," says Margit Bella.

"Ay, an' the oul sayin' has it—

> If you rub it on wood
> It's sure to come good.

Ses Teeshie.

"That's rite," ses Sally Ann, "An'

> If ye rub it on brass
> It will come to pass."

Another energetic young lady who should succeed in life, announced:—

> "I can bake, I can sew, I can darn,
> And what I don't know I'm willing to larn."

To conclude with a word of advice to bachelors:—

> "Find the girl that's orderly,
> She is the household treasure,
> Never mind the parlour bright,
> But watch the kitchen dresser."

CHAPTER XXIV.

General Sayings.

Amongst the sayings in popular use in the countryside is "**As black as Toal's cloak**," to designate anything particularly dirty or discoloured. The origin of this saying has never been cleared up, and the following suggested explanation may stand until such times as a more authoritative one is given.

A.D. 76, Tuathal Teachtmhar—Tuathal the Legitimate became monarch of Ireland. He had two daughters, Dairine and Fithir, the most accomplished and handsome young ladies in Ireland. The King of Leinster sought and obtained the elder sister in marriage; but for some reason or reasons known only to himself, he repented of this step less than a year after their union. He therefore went to her father's palace at Tara, and with a sorrowful countenance, told King Tuathal that his daughter Dairine was dead, and earnestly implored him to bestow upon him her younger sister as the only means of repairing his grievous loss.

King Tuathal complied with his request and the fair princess Fithir was delivered to the King of Leinster, who conveyed her to his palace. On her arrival she found Dairine alive. Overcome with grief and shame she died instantly. The distracted Dairine threw herself upon the lifeless body of her sister and also expired. When King Tuathal heard of the death of his children he called his nobles and their followers together, marched into Leinster with fire and sword, and after committing dreadful havoc, he compelled Eochaid and his unfortunate people to bind themselves to a solemn engagement to pay him and his successors forever a chief rent or tax called **Borumha-Laighean**. This tax was paid in cattle, silver, etc., besides three score hundred mantles or cloaks. (O'Connor's *Keating*,[19] pp. 237-9, ed. 1854.) The tribute was ordered to be disposed of in this manner:—A third part of it was to be paid to the people of Oirgiallach (mid-Ulster), a third part to the inhabitants of Conacht, and the remaining part to Jobh Neill. This tax was actually paid every second year during the reigns of forty of King Tuathal's successors. Thus, for some centuries these mantles or cloaks were regularly sent to the north of Ireland, and it is not to be wondered at that they soon became known as Tuathal's (pronounced Thool, or Tool— *anglice* Toal) cloaks. Then, as to the colour, Giraldus Cambrensis says that in his time "the Irish were but lightly clad in woollen garments, barbarously shaped, for the most part black, because the sheep of that country are black."

The Scottish Highlanders dyed their garments tartan and purple, or as near the heather tint as possible; and the Irish, for the same reason, as the bogs were their constant retreat. (Ledwich, p. 339. Borlase's *Irish Rebellion*, p. 75).

Again we read that "the Irish dye their garments black with the bark of trees called by the English alders (Gough's *Camden's Brittanica*, III., 658)." From these and other writers it may be inferred that the cloaks sent into Ulster were black, and as these were distributed to the lesser chiefs and people gratis, would soon pass into a proverb or saying.

"**A Miller's Lift**" is a term used by quarrymen and millwrights. This is the upward lift of the handle of the crowbar. Prise is the downward push of the handle end. The phrase originated in the fact that the grinding surfaces of millstones in use become worn and require to be redressed from time to time. To do this the upper stone is raised until it stands on its edge, by placing the lower end of the iron bar on the nether millstone as a fulcrum, while an upward motion is given to the hand at the higher end; a downward motion being inapplicable in this case. In a "Miller's Lift" the crow, or iron bar, acts as a lever of the second order; in a prise it is a lever of the first order. The writer has noted the phrase in the counties of Antrim and Tyrone, and is doubtless used elsewhere.

"**It's all over like the fair of Athy**" is said of a matter ending almost as soon as begun. A north of Ireland form is "It's all over like a hunt."

"**I'll die where Bradley died, in the middle of the bed**," i.e., at home and happy.

"**A rag upon every bush**." This saying is usually applied to young men who are in the habit of paying attention to more than one young lady at a time—"Oh, so-and-so has a rag on every bush," and has its origin in the custom of affixing shreds of rag to the hawthorn trees which almost invariably stand on the brink of Irish holy wells. The idea is that the putting up of these rags is a putting away of the evils impending or incurred by sin, an act accompanied by the following ritual words:—"By the intercession of the Lord I leave my portion of illness on this place." (W. C. Borlase—"Rag Offerings and Primitive Pilgrimages in Ireland": *Athenæum*, 1st April, 1893). A devotee, or *voteen* as they would be called, going from one holy well and its particular saint to another, would have but little love for his own local saint and his rag would hang on many a bush, hence the saying.

In Ireland when a person wishes to postpone some matter indefinitely, the promise is to do it on "**Tibb's Eve.**" To the uninitiated, if there be any such, this festival comes "neither before nor after Christmas." Whether the Irish "Tibb," whose eve is referred to, has any connection with St. Tibba, the Saxon saint, whose day is December 14th, is a matter for ecclesiastical antiquaries to determine. Other places have equivalent sayings, such as "The Greek Kalends," "when two Sundays meet," "to-morrow come never."

According to a south of Ireland legend, St. Patrick, on one occasion, used a very similar evasion. As the story goes, there was a great serpent that infested the district where Bruff now is. St. Patrick drove the serpent into Lough Gur, and "commanded" it to remain there until the Easter Monday before Judgment Day. Ever since, the serpent comes up to the surface of the lough on Easter Monday once in seven years, and asks in Irish: "How is it, O Patrick! from that last Monday?" or literally, "How long is it, O Patrick, from that Monday at the end of time?" In County Wexford they have the saying, "**put a nick in the post.**" The same phrase obtains in the north of Ireland, but in the longer form of "put a nick in the post with a wooden hatchet," but there the origin of the saying is forgotten. Patrick Kennedy, in "Evenings in the Duffrey" (p. 64), thus explains how it arose:—"Leaving the two bedrooms below the parlour uninspected, we return to the kitchen. The everlasting settle lies along the wall opposite the door. A strong beam resting in a hole in this wall, its other end supported by the entrance partition wall, bears up the huge structure of the projecting chimney. A post supporting this beam gets a nick whenever anything unusual takes place, such as Owen passing the day without telling some tremendous lie; or Harry, the eldest son, tying the thongs (laces) of his shoes of a morning. Within the shelter of this capacious chimney, all the family may easily sit without the fear of striking their heads should they stand up."

A saying common over Ireland to indicate some event happening either at a very distant period, or not at all, is—"**It will be when the devil goes blind, and he's not bleared yet**," or in a slightly different form—"It will be when the devil is blind, but he has not got sore eyes yet," which is the same thing, but not in such dialectic form. This saying probably came from Scotland, as in "Guy Mannering," Ch. XXII., Tib. Mumps says:—"There's no ane in Bewcastle would do the like o' that now—we be a true folk now." To which Dandie replies, "Ay, Tib, that will be when the de'il's blind, and his een's no sair yet."

Another saying applied to the organ of sight is, when referring to a glass of whiskey of extra strong or good quality, that "**it would take the pearl off a piper's eye**." The pearl was, and possibly is still, in provincial talk, the white, cloud-like film that forms on part or parts of the cornea of the eye as a result of disease. Therefore the quality of the liquor was so potent as to clear off the film and cause the blind person to see. In former times it was not unusual to train as harpers persons who had lost their sight. Carolan[20] being a particularly illustrious example, and as in these degenerate days the race of harpers has passed away, the alliterative word "piper" was used, because they, like "blind fiddlers," also followed a calling that could be pursued by those bereft of sight, and readers will not need to be reminded of John Keegan's "Coach, the Piper," one of the most charming of Irish poems, in which he tells us how—

> "One winter's day, long, long ago,
>   When I was a little fellow;
> A piper wandered to our door,
>   Grey-headed, blind and yellow."

"**Sweat like a brock**." This common saying is very misleading. Brock, as everyone knows, is the Gaelic name for a badger, and is quite as often used as the English name, but why this animal should be used as a symbol for a state of extreme perspiration would be indeed difficult to explain. In fact it is not connected at all with the Irish *broc*, a badger, but with the English dialect word (common in several of the shires) for the larva of the frog-hopper or cuckoo-spit insect, sometimes called the "sweating insect," and known to entomologists as the *cicada spumata* (the foamy cicada). Therefore, any person or animal sweating like a brock would be covered with a foamy lather similar to the familiar cuckoo-spit.

"**The curse of the crows**" has been considered by some writers to arise from a superstition among Irish peasantry that, when crows desert their habitation adjoining a dwelling-house or castle, it signifies that the owner will be the last of his race: hence if your property is abandoned by this feathered tribe, it is a bad omen, the expression being equivalent to "May your family become extinct." A newspaper writer claims the phrase as a Cork one, on the authority of the following related by an old resident:—"In 1796 the fine old elm trees which from time immemorial overshadowed the burial ground of St. Anne Shandon, were cut down by the then rector, Mr. Hyde, and sold to the timber merchant. The crows (the popular name for rooks) had a settlement, and when they were evicted many of them (presumably fledglings) perished. The neighbours pitied the poor birds, and thus the term in question came to be used in Blarney Lane and its neighbourhood." (*Jour. Cork Hist. and Archl. Soc.*, 1st Ser., I., 48.)

"**There's a hole in the ballad**." This saying is applied to persons who suffer from a lapse of memory when relating an incident or occurrence. The phrase had its origin in bygone days when street ballads supplied the place of newspapers, and the rustics who purchased them in fairs and markets, carried them in their pockets until they were worn into holes and partially illegible, in the north of England the phrase is "a piece torn out of a ballad."

"**There never was a gant but there was a want**." Gant is an old word for yawn, and yawning usually indicates fatigue or want of sleep.

"Elegance and ease, like a shoeblack in a noddy."
This is a Dublin saying, and the vehicle in question is described in Bush's "Hibernia Curiosa, a letter from a gentleman in Dublin to his friend at Dover," pp. 23-24, London, 1769. It is, however, more graphically delineated by a later writer. "The Ringsend car" was succeeded by the "noddy," so called from its oscillating movement backwards and forwards. It was a low vehicle, capable of holding two persons, and drawn by one horse. It was covered with a calash, open before, but the aperture was usually filled by the "noddy-boy," who was generally a large sized man, and occupied a seat that protruded back, so that he sat in the lap of his company. The use of the vehicle by certain classes grew into a proverb—"Elegance and ease like a shoeblack in a noddy." (*Ireland Sixty Years Ago*, p. 70, Dublin 1847). The noddy took its name from the motion of the driver, whose feet rested on the shafts of the vehicle, and who, when the horse was trotting, went nod, nod, nodding. It became extinct about the year eighteen twenty.

"There is reason in roasting eggs." No eggs are cooked by roasting nowadays, except by youngsters. It was not so in Shakespeare's time, for Touchstone says "Truly thou art damned; like an ill roasted egg, all on one side." ("As You Like It," A. 2, Sc. III.)

"The long eleventh of June." This term used to be applied to the eleventh of June in the belief that it was a very long day, if not the longest in the year. The origin of the expression, which has survived, must be, of course, referred back to a period prior to the reform of the calendar, which was adopted by Act of Parliament in 1752, by which eleven days were struck out, thus the old style 11th June became the 22nd June. Rhyme heard in County Tyrone many years ago runs:—

> "Buttermilk Antony, but that's a mournful tune,
> And the dung in the dunghill in the long 'leventh of June."

This would be said to an individual who was idling away his time, whistling or singing some old "Come all ye" at a time when the potato crop should be in the ground, or the planting in active operation. There is an old rhyme common in Lancashire:—

"Barnaby Bright,
    All day and no night."

Before the reformation of the calendar the festival of St. Barnabas fell on the 11th June.

In the county of Kildare a very tall person is described as being "as long as the eleventh of June," while a mean wretch would "steal the cross off an ass," and a drunken man is said to be "up in his hat." "A broth of a boy" may have originated in the Irish *broth*, passion. Brotha: passionate, spirited, its meaning being he's a lad of spirit.

In County Antrim, and it may be in other parts, there is a saying—"The thing is quite correct, the child's name is Anthony, and the woman must get her ducks." In the West Riding of Yorkshire it takes the form of "All's well that ends well, and t' child's name is Anthony." In other parts it is "The berrin's (burying) gone by and t' child's called Anthony."

CHAPTER XXV.

General Sayings continued.

"Joy be with him and a bottle of moss." In this case the word bottle has no connection with the domestic vessel so familiar to us all, being derived from the old French *botel*, diminutive of *bot*, a bundle. A common expression for a hopeless search is:—"as well look for a needle in a bottle of hay," which in more literary, though less forcible form, would be "like searching for a needle in a haystack." The earliest mention given in the *Oxford Dictionary* is under the year 1386:—"Al-though it be nat worth a Botel hey." Chaucer: "Prologue to Manciple's Tale," I., 14. A later illustration is "Methinks I have a great desire to a bottle of hay." Shakespeare: "Midsummer Night's Dream," IV., I. The saying at the head of the paragraph hails from County Derry and is a good example of an English word long since obsolete, still preserved in current Ulster speech.

The writer has been unable to obtain any explanation of the following sayings:—

"As great a liar as the clock of Strabane." Evidently the public clock of that town must have been a very unreliable timekeeper.

"He is singing whillelujah to the day nettles." This possibly refers to a lazy farmer or labourer who is idling away his time instead of being busy. It is a North of Ireland expression.

"He is as great a liar as Oram." This is a common County Louth saying, and it would be of interest to know who this distinguished disciple of Ananias was, and how he distinguished himself as a prevaricator.

"A handstaff of holly, a builtin (soople) of hazel, a single sheaf, and a clean floor" (Ulster Gaelic saying).

"The good horses come from Armagh, and the pretty girls from the county Down" (Ulster Gaelic saying).

"Like Johnny Weir, what he doesn't like he doesn't hear."

"As stiff as Paddy's father that died in the frost."

"Short and dark like a winter's day."

"Sit on your heel and thank goodness for a new stool." Said to anyone finding difficulty in getting a seat.

"The backside of God speed, where the mare foaled the fiddler." This phrase is sometimes used to indicate the place of residence of the hero and heroine of a fairy or folk tale. 'Backside' is an old word indicating the back portion of the premises belonging to a dwelling-house—the yard and garden. It is now obsolete in Armagh and Tyrone, but may still be heard occasionally in Antrim and Down.

"Begrudged meat would not fatten a pig." (Co. Down.)

"Forty things to do and bread to bake." (Co. Tyrone.)

"May you live long and wear a watch," as they say in county Sligo.

> "When the bouchalawn wears a heavy head,
> Mow low the mead." (Wexford.)

When weeds show a great quantity of seeds it is a sign of a severe winter, hence the necessity of providing plenty of fodder.

"A sloe year, a woe year."

When sloes are plentiful a hard year is expected.

"A haw year, a braw year."

"Don't be breaking your shin on a stool that's not in your way." This is equivalent to the English saying of—"Betty Baxter, that refused a man before he ax'd her."

"'Tis often the lad with the ten overtakes the man with the forty."

"Where food is scarce the taste is sweet."

"Don't take the thatch off your own house to buy slates for another man's roof."

"As cute as a pet fox."

"May the Lord keep you in his hand and never close his fist too tight on you."

The late W. H. Patterson, of Belfast, who was an accomplished antiquary and folk-lorist, noted down the following: —

Duck Proverbs.

"As yellow as a duck's foot." Alluding to the complexion usually, but might be applied to anything of a very yellow hue.

"You're a foother[21] an' the ducks will get you." This is said to a silly blundering person.

"Take it in your hand and throw it to the ducks." Advice given for the disposal of something worthless.

"A fine day for young ducks." A wet day. It is also a common English saying.

"Turn up your eyes like a duck in thunder." Said of a person always dying and dwaming and turning up their eyes at things. The Yorkshire form of this saying is—"To dark like a duck in thunder." That is, to draw the inner membrane over the eye. This membrane is a provision of nature for the protection of the duck's eyes when diving or foraging for food under the water.

"Crutches for lame ducks." When a person is asked what he is making and does not wish to tell, he replies "crutches for lame ducks."

"What Barney shot at the lough." This is what unsuccessful sportsmen who return empty-handed are said to have got, with generally the added phrase, "Sweet d— all." Barney must have been as bad a shot as "wee Mr. Anthony," the would-be sportsman of Lynn Doyle's stories.

They have a similar saying in Munster.

"We're burying what the Connaught man shot at—nothing."

It is said of any particularly winning or attractive person that they could "coax cold potatoes off a dresser."

"All in a lump like Brown's cows."

"All gab and guts like a young cow." This is said of a forward, talkative child.

"It's as broad as it's long, like Paddy's blanket." In the blanket trade what are known as "Irish sizes" are more nearly square than those made for the English trade, which are made longer in order that they tuck under the mattress at the foot of the bed.

"Don't be putting in your cutty among spoons." Said to a child joining on its own initiative in the conversation of its elders.

"The devil couldn't do it unless he was drunk." Said of something very difficult of accomplishment.

"The deil go with you and sixpence, then you'll want neither money nor company."

"I'll give you what Paddy gave the drum," i.e., a good beating.

"You're like the woman's peas, lost for a roddin'." Said to a spoilt, badly trained child.

CHAPTER XXVI.

Riddles.

In the history of civilisation riddles stand near to proverbs, and the two travel on long together, being still to be found among the upper savage races, and on the lower and middle ranges of civilisation. In days when folk-lore and literature were oral, riddles played no inconsiderable part in passing the time when the family assembled around the fireside of a winter's night, or the neighbours gathered in for a *ceilidh*. Boys being "young barbarians," many of the ancient specimens have lasted on in the school and by the cottage fireside through their agency, that otherwise would have been forgotten by their elders. There is a wealth of both proverbs and riddles in the Gaelic language which lie outside the scope of the present work, and still await adequate record and treatment. The following examples, therefore, are Anglo-Irish riddles which have largely been neglected by Irish antiquaries and folk-lorists. The only papers dealing with the subject known to the writer being one in the "Gentleman's Magazine" for the year 1880, entitled "About Riddles," by David Fitzgerald, which deals with those of all countries, including a few Irish. The other is a very interesting paper by P. J. M'Call, in the "Journal of the National Literary Society of Ireland," Vol. II., Part II., 1900, which deals with "Folk-lore Riddles, Irish and Anglo-Irish." With the Gaelic riddles as already mentioned, it is not intended to deal, but there are quite a number of cases in which old Gaelic riddles that may have been in vogue when Finn MacCool and his Fenian bands hunted the hills of Erin, have been translated into English, and so travelled down the social stream with no change beyond that of from one language to another, possibly as the Gaelic of a given district was replaced by English speech. The specimens of riddles that follow are from the writer's collection and recollection, supplemented by others from the papers already referred to. It spoils the effect of the riddles to give the answer along with them, but there is no other convenient way.

> "Chip, chip, cherry,
> There isn't a man in Derry
> Can catch chip, chip, cherry."

Answer: Smoke.

> "Here I have it and yonder I see it,
> A black lamb with blue feet."

Answer: The breath on a frosty day.

The following is more in the nature of a catch than a riddle:—

> "In mudeelis, in claynonis,
> In boharis, in seanonis."

Interpretation:

> In mud eel is, in clay none is,
> In bush hare is, in sea none is.

Another catchy one is:—

> "The fifer and his wife, the fiddler and his mother,
> Ate three half cakes, three whole cakes, and three-quarters
> of another."

This is by no means the formidable problem in vulgar fractions that it seems. It is quite simple when we know that the party consisted of three persons only, the fiddler being the son of the fifer and his wife, therefore they ate a cake and three-quarters each.

Another little genealogical riddle that some people can interpret as soon as they hear it, and others find difficult—the writer remembers a couple of the senior classes in a country school rhyming it over for several days before they hit upon the answer—is:—

> "Teague's father was Donald's grandfather,
> What relation was Teague to Donald?"

Answer: Teague was Donald's father.

Another form in which it is sometimes given is:—

"Jack's father was John's son,
   How near akin was Jack to John?"

Answer: Jack was John's grandson.

Another variation of the same subject is:—

"A man being asked what relation a little boy was to him, replied:—

   'Sisters or brothers I never had one,
      Yet that little boy's father was my father's son.'"

Answer:—The little boy was his son.

   "What kin is that child to its own father,
      Who is not its father's son?"

Answer: Daughter.

   "Down in my garden I have a beaufat (buffet),
      And four-and-twenty carpenters working at that,
      Some have blue bonnets and some have straw hats,
      Come riddle me that?"

Answer: A hive of bees.

   "There was a man who had no eyes,
      And he went out to view the skies;
      He saw a tree with apples on,
      He took none off, and he left none on."

Answer: A man with one eye went out and saw a tree with two apples upon it, one of which he took and left the other.

   "One moonlight night as I sat high,
      I watched for one and two passed by;
      The leaves did shake, the earth did quake,
      To see the hole the fox did make."

Answer: A man murdered his sweetheart, then dug a hole and buried her at the foot of the tree.

The foregoing was picked up by the writer when a boy in his native county Tyrone, amongst much other material classed as rubbish by his wiser seniors. In after years he was to come across it when reading Quiller Couch's fine story, "The Astonishing History of Troy Town" [Fowey, Cornwall], Chap. XIX.

"Et puts me in mind," he went on as his master was silent, "o' th' ould lidden [a monotonous chant or burden] as us used to sing when us was tiny mites:—

> Riddle me, riddle me right,
> Where was I last Sat'rday night?
> I seed a chimp-champ champin' at his bridle,
> I seed an ould fox workin' hissel' idle.
> The trees did shever, an' I did shake,
> To see the hole thic' fox did make."

"What is it every living man has seen and never more will see again?"

Answer: Yesterday.

"What is born in winter, dies in the summer, and grows with its root upwards?"

Answer: An icicle.

> "As I went out, as I went in,
> I saw the dead that the life was in;
> The sixth sat, the seventh flew,
> Riddle me that or hanged you'll be."

Answer: A bird's nest in a dead horse's skull.

"My mistress sent me to your mistress for the loan of the hiddick, the haddick, the double cannadic, and you'll get your share of the whirligig."

Answer: A child sent by one teacher to another teacher for the loan of a cane.

"What is short and cut a piece off it and it will make it longer?"

Answer: A grave.

> "Look in your hand and you'll plainly see
> What never was, nor never will be."

Answer: The little finger never was, nor never will be as long as the fourth finger.

> "My face is black, yet much admired.
> And ladies and gentlemen sit by me till they're tired.
> They take me up, and break my head, and cut my face,
> And throw me out of my dwelling-place."

Answer: The fire.

The following is a combination of two riddles:—

> "Blackie sat upon redie,
> And redie made blackie's inside grumble."

Answer: Fire making a pot boil.

Here is an old favourite:—

> "Riddle me, riddle me, randy bow,
> My father gave me seed to sow;
> The seed was black, and the ground was white,
> Riddle me that and I'll give you a pipe."

Answer: Ink and writing paper.

> "What is it that is neither flesh nor bone,
> Yet has four fingers and a thumb?"

Answer: A glove.

"Passing through a guttery gap" seems to be a favourite way of commencing a riddle. Here is a group of them.

> "As I went through a guttery gap,
> I met a wee man with a red cap;
> A stick in his stern, a stone in his belly,
> Riddle me that and I'll give you a penny."

Answer: A haw.

> "As I went through yon guttery gap,
>   I met my uncle Davy;
> I cut off his head and drunk his blood,
>   And left his body aisy."

Answer: A bottle of whiskey.

There is a very similar Scottish riddle to the foregoing:—

> "As I cam' ower Stirlin' brig,
>   I met wi' George Bowhannan;
> I took off his head and drank his blude,
>   An' left his body stannin'."

Answer: A bottle of whiskey.

George Buchanan was jester to James I. of England.

"How long would you live and eat nothing but stirabout? If you eat nothing, in a very short time you wouldn't be able to stir about.

> "There was a man, was no man,
> He had a gun, was no gun,
> He shot a bird, and no bird,
> Upon a tree, and no tree."

Answer: A boy with a pop-gun shot a butterfly upon a holly bush.

> "Little Jenny Whiteskin—she has a red nose,
> The longer she lives, the shorter she grows."

Answer: A candle.

> "As round as an apple, as deep as a cup,
>   And all the king's horses wouldn't drag it up."

Answer: A well.

> "As round as a pear, as deep as a pail—
>   If you want me to talk, you must pull my tail."

Answer: A bell.

"I go under the water, and over the water,
And cry "Chink, chink!" yet never take a drink."

Answer: A fetter on a horse's foot.

"I go round the land, and round the land,
And sleep at night on my head."

Answer: A nail in a brogue.

"I go round the house, and round the house,
Upstairs and downstairs,
And sleep in a corner at night."

Answer: A besom.

"As I went over Cairney hill,
Cairney hill was shaking,
Four and twenty wee things,
All stark naked.
The hindmost was foremost,
The foremost was hindmost,
And they were all stone blind."

Answer: The spokes in a cart wheel.

A riddle that requires considerable powers of penetration amongst youngsters is the following:—

"There was a man rode through this town,
Great Grizzle was his name;
His saddle it was gilt with gold,
And yet I cannot tell his name—
But now three times I've told his name."

Answer: Was.

"Down in yon dark dungeon there is a bright knight,
All saddled, all bridled, all ready for fight;
If you can't name him, it is a great shame,
For thrice have I named his name."

Answer: All.

"Says the King to the King, call the dog after,
Says the King to the King, what shall I call him?
Says the King to the King, thrice have I named him."

Answer: Says.

"The King of Morocco he built a ship,
An' in that ship his daughter sits;
An' I tell her name, I am to blame,
An' there's three times I've told her name."

Answer: An(n).

"The King of Morocco he sent to Queen Anne,
For a bottomless vessel to put flesh and blood in."

Answer: A ring.

"An iron grey with a flaxen tail,
And a brass boy driving it."

Answer: Needle, thread, and thimble.

"As I went over yonder stile,
I met a thing that carried me a mile;
The cow calved it, the goose laid it,
It grew in a wood, and a smith made, it."

Answer: A saddle, it being composed of leather, feathers, wood and iron.

"As I looked out of my gay gold window,
I dropped my gay gold ring;
I saw the dead carrying the living,
Wasn't that a wonderful thing?"

Answer: A ship.

This riddle the writer picked up along with much other equally useful information in boyhood days in Tyrone and in Mr. M'Call's paper there is given an almost word for word translation of the Gaelic original.

> "O'er the gravel I do travel,
>   On the oak tree I do stand—
> I ride a mare that never was foaled,
>   And hold the bridle in my hand."

Answer: A sailor on a ship.

> "White fowl feather-less
> Flew from Paradise—
> Perched upon the castle wall,
> Out came Lord John Landless,
> Shot it handless,
> Rode away horseless,
> To the king's white hall,
> Just before my eyes."

Answer: Snow and sun.

> "Behind my heel, behind my house,
> There is a grey mare and her coult,
> The king and all his men couldn't
> Turn that grey mare's tail about."

Answer: The moon.

Rev. Canon Courtnay Moore, M.A., in a sketch of "Jacky Barrett," the famous Vice-Provost of T.C.D. (*Jour. Cork H. & A. Soc.*, Ser. II., V., VI., p. 51), quotes a riddle given by him to an undergraduate:—

"Come, sir, I'll give you a riddle, do you see me, in honour of Christmas."

> "Take five from five, and into its place,
>   Put twice five hundred and fifty;
> 'Twill show you a thing that out of its case
>   Will many a caper give ye."

"After a little time he said: 'Well, can't you guess it, sir? Well, then, come here, and I'll tell it to you. If you take V., which is the numeral letter for five, and put two D's and L., which stand for 1,050, in its place, then it will be fiddle; and don't you think that would make you caper, you see?'" It is a pity Charles Lever did not know of this riddle of "Jacky Barrett's," as, if he had he would most likely have made him propound it to either Frank Webber of lively memory, or "Charles O'Malley."

> "The bat, the bee, the butterfly,
> The laverock[22] and the lark,
> The heather bleat, the mire snipe,
> How many birds is that?"

Answer: Two.

A variant of it is:—

> "The cuckoo and the gowk,[23]
> The laverock and the lark,
> The heather-bleat and the mire snipe,
> How many birds is that?"

Answer: Three.

> "Out of the West there grew a thing:
> The Queen could not ride it, neither could the King.
> They sent for a wise man out of the East—
> He swore it had horns and it wasn't a beast."

Answer: A holly bush.

CHAPTER XXVII.

Riddles continued.

"High behind and low before,
    Riddle me that and I'll tell you more?"

Answer: A salt box.

"Everything has it and so has a needle."

Answer: A name.

"Londonderry, Cork and Kerry,
    Spell that without a K?"

Answer: T.h.a.t.

"Eliza, Elizabeth, Betty, and Bess,
    Went to the wood to seek a bird's nest.
    In it they found four eggs—
    Each took one, how many eggs were left?"

Answer: Three.

"As I went to Finglush, I met a whin bush,
    And when I came back it was elder."

Answer: Older.

"Two dead men fighting,
    Two blind men looking on,
    Two cripples running for the police,
    Two dummies saying 'hurry on.' "

Answer: A lie.

"As black as ink, as white as milk—
    Hops on the ground like hailstones."

Answer: A magpie.

"The man that made it never wore it,
    The man that wore it never saw it."

Answer: A coffin.

"There was a man of Adam's race,
   Had a certain dwelling place;
   He lived neither on earth, heaven, or hell,
   Tell me where he did dwell?"

Answer: Jonah in the whale's belly.

"I have but one horn, I'm no unicorn,
   I'm milked, but I'm no Kerry cow;
   My grandmother loves me, and on the fire shoves me,
   With smiling good looks on her brow."

Answer: A teapot.

"Old mother Twitchet had but one eye,
   And a long tail that she let fly.
   Every time she passes a gap
   A piece of her tail gets caught in the trap."

Answer: A needle and thread.

"I have a wee brown cow, she stands by the wall,
   Give her much, give her little, she will eat it all.
   Give her air she will fly, give her water she will die."

Answer: The fire.

"It is round and sound, and just a pound, and barely half an ounce."

Answer: A Sovereign.

"I went to wood for a wee piece of timber;
   It was neither crooked nor straight, or the length of your
      finger."

Answer: A nut.

"It grows in the wood and sounds in the town,
   And earns its master many a pound."

Answer: A fiddle.

"A duck before two ducks, and a duck behind two ducks, and a duck
      in the middle."

Answer: Three.

> "Long-legged father, big-bellied mother,
> Three wee children, one not a hair bigger than the other."

Answer: The pot and pot-hooks.

"Water will wash it, but sun won't dry it."

Answer: Butter.

"What goes round the house, and round the house, and a harrow after it?"

Answer: A hen and a flock of chickens.

"What goes round the wood and never goes into the wood?"

Answer: A cat licking a butter tub.

"Why is a pig in a parlour like a house on fire?"

Answer: Because you be trying to put both out.

"What sleeps with its finger in its eye?"

Answer: The crook.

> "Long legs, crooked thighs,
> Wee head and no eyes."

Answer: The tongs.

> "Niddy Noddy, wee black body,
> Three feet and a wooden hat."

Answer: A pot.

"Niddy Noddy, two heads, one body."

Answer: A reel.

"Black and white, and re[a]d all over."

Answer: A newspaper.

"Why is Ireland like a bottle?"

Answer: Because it has a Cork in the end of it.

"As I was going by yon demesne wall,
  I met a man and he gave a loud call;
  His beard was flesh, and his mouth was horn,
  And such a man was never born."

Answer: A rooster.

"Head without hair, teeth without lips,
  Long tail and no hips."

Answer: A rake.

"What goes through the fields with my father's coat on its back?"

Answer: A sheep.

"Spell a red running rogue with three letters."

Answer: F.o.x.

"Spell blind pig with two letters."

Answer: P.g.

How is that? Because if you put an i in it, it would see.

"The length of your arm, and as black as a coal,
  The nearer the stern the wider the hole."

Answer: A stocking.

"There is an old woman who lives in a ditch,
  And if you go near her she'll give you an itch."

Answer: A nettle.

"I went away between two woods, and came home between two waters."

Answer: A "go" of water.

Wooden buckets were in general use until superseded by zinc buckets, during the latter half of the nineteenth century.

"Blackety sat upon rickety,
  Glowery soon spied that—

Handed it over to grabbety,
Can you riddle me that?"

Answer: Gathering a blackberry.

"Four down hangers, four straight standers,
Two hookers, two lookers, a switcher and a licker."

Answer: A cow.

"Wee Jinny Ruddle, she sits in a puddle,
With a white petticoat, an' a green gown."

Answer: A rush.

"As I went over Westminster bridge,
I met a Westminster scholar—
I took out my pipe an' drew on my gloves,
Now tell me the name of the scholar."

Answer: Andrew.

"As I sat upon my hunkers,
Lookin' through my winkers,
I saw the dead burying the living."

Answer: Raking a turf fire before going to bed.

"It's long and it's narrow, an' not very wide,
An' wears a green selvidge on every side."

Answer: The road.

"What's full and holds more?"

Answer: A pot of potatoes.

"As I went over Corney hill
Corney hill was quakin',
Four and twenty wee things
All bare naked.
With a bell in his bosom,
An' a bonnie wee white hat,
If you guessed till Sunday
You wouldn't guess that."

Answer: A field of daisies.

> "As I went through yon guttery gap,
>   I met my aunty Mary;
>   She had timber toes and eyes and nose,
>   Upon my word she would frighten the crows."

(County Cork.) Answer: A gun.

The following is the Tyrone version of the above riddle:—

> "As I went down yonder lane I met my aunt Eliza Jane.
>   Her heel was brass, her cheek was brown,
>   The longest leg in Corney town;
>   An' iron nose an' timber toes,
>   An' I declare she'd scare the crows."

Answer: A gun.

> "In Mornigan's park there is a deer,
>   Silver horns and golden ear—
>   Neither fish, flesh, feather, nor bone,
>   In Mornigan's park she walks alone."

(Leinster.) Answer: The moon.

> "In Sampson's park there is a deer,
>   And day and night it doth appear.
>   It's neither flesh, body, blood, nor bone,
>   In Sampson's park it stands alone."

(County Tyrone.) Answer: A deer's statue.

"Willie the Duck, speaking in a quivering voice, began to ask riddles:

"What bears but never blossoms?" he enquired.

"The hangman's rope," was the answer.

"What tree never comes to fruit?" he asked.

"The gallows tree," was the answer.

"This is the best guess to-night," said Willie, taking a pinch of snuff and sneezing violently. "No one will be able to answer it. . .

'In the morning four legs; at noon two legs; in the evening three legs, and at night four legs; what would that be?"

"It's a man." said Eamon Doherty, looking round with a triumphant glance. "In his young days a man walks on his hands and knees, when he grows up he walks on two legs; when he gets old he walks on three legs, two and a stick; and if he lives long enough he'll walk on crutches, God be good to us! that's four legs."

"You're a man with a head, Eamon," said Willie the Duck. (County Donegal.) Patrick MacGill: *The Rat-Pit*, Chapter IX. "The wake of James Ryan."

"Now, boys," said the volunteer teacher, "take slates and cutters [slate pencils], and write out this word:—

> "Three-fourths of a cross and a circle complete,
> Two semi-circles and a perpendicular meet,
> Then set a triangle on two feet,
> Two semi-circles and a circle complete."

Answer: TOBACCO.

. . . And now I'll be off after you get this question copied down, and maybe I won't do anything for whoever shows it clear and cleanly made up this day week:—

> "A man there was that bought a horse,
>   And he was lean and poor,
> One guinea sterling was his price,
>   And five bright shillings more.
> He fed this horse on hay and oats
>   Until he got right sound;
> And meeting with another chap,
>   He sold him for five pound.
> One half he lost of his prime cost,
>   One fourth his keeping too;
> What did his fodder stand him in?
>   What did he lose? say you."

"And any little boy that can find the answer may try doing this little one while he is resting himself.

> "Money lent at five per cent.
>   To those who choose to borrow;
> What time shall I be worth a pound
>   If I lend a crown to-morrow?"

The school at Rathnure, county Wexford, about 1817, from Patrick Kennedy's "The Banks of the Boro," p. 260.

> "Two brothers we are, great burdens we bear,
>   We are full all day and empty when we go to rest."

Answer: A pair of shoes.

"What is the shortest bridge in the world?"

Answer: The bridge of the nose.

> "What is it that man can see every day,
>   And God never sees?"

Answer: A greater than himself.

In conclusion, here are a couple of riddles, one partly solved, the other unsolved. Can any reader guess them? The writer does not know the answers.

> "As I went up the hill of Killiblunder,
>   I saw twenty-four blackbirds tearing the ground asunder,
>   A cat lighting a candle, a mouse chasing a deer,
>   And if you're a good scholar, riddle me that in a year."

The answer to the first portion is "the pins in a harrow." The remainder is unsolved.

This is the unsolved one which was given by a boy in Westmeath:—

> "Last Saturday night I drank a drink
>   Through a gold ring in a glass window wall,
>   And that's a riddle among yez all."

A suggested answer is:—"A man drinking who is wearing gold rimmed glasses."

CHAPTER XXVIII.

War cries of the Irish septs and Anglo-Irish barons.

With a fighting race such as the Irish, when in bygone days every provincial king and petty chieftain was a law unto himself and settled his real or imaginary wrongs, as well as enforced his rights literally by the **Lamh Laidir** (strong arm), the war cry was a necessity. Distinctive uniforms such as are worn by soldiers in modern warfare did not obtain with the Irish, who all dressed alike in the saffron-coloured linen shirt. They were therefore compelled to use distinguishing words in the day of battle in order to recognise friends from foes. The **gairm sluiagh** (battle cry) was at the beginning of the conflict a charging shout, the slogan, insignium, or vocal banner on each side, besides which every clan had a visible ensign in the standard, round which it rallied.

In all encounters the use of "Farrah, Farrah!" was common. Feara, or more probably "Faire," an admonition to those who were about to take care, like the French "Gare-a-vous." "Aboo" is another word universally used as the termination of battle cries, but has neither meaning as a word nor federal significance as a slogan.

The cry generally used was the name of the chief, or of a renowned ancestor, or the name of the gathering place or headquarters of the clan, and when the mode of fighting changed, these cries were laid aside, or transferred as mottoes to the crests of families using them.

One of the most famous in Irish annals is that of the O'Neills, Dynasts of Ulster—"Lamh-dearg-aboo!"—the Red hand, which was the O'Neill cognizance borne on their banner. According to a list given in Camden of the O'Neill retinue that went to England with Shane-an-Diomais, M'Caffrey was his standard-bearer. Clan Caffrey were a branch of the Maguires, who took the district surname of MacCaffrey. This name is still numerous in County Fermanagh.

The neighbouring and rival clan of O'Donnell, of Tir-connell, had for their war-cry, "O'Donnell-aboo!" and well might their bards adjure the fighting men of the clan as they followed the "Cathach," or "Battle Book" of the O'Donnells into the fray:—

> "Sons of Tir-connaill, all valiant and true!
> Make the false Saxons feel
> Erin's avenging steel—
> Strike for your country—'O'Donnell abu'!"

Other war cries of Northern clans still on record are "Battail'lah-aboo!" used by the M'Swynes, of Donegal. They were gallowglasses, or battle-axe men, and their cry alluded to these heavy armed soldiers who formed the main body, or "battle" as it used to be termed of the army.

"Keartlevarry-aboo!" The ball of tow yarn, which they probably wore as a distinguishing badge, was the battle-cry of the M'Kennas, of Truagh, County Monaghan.

"Ardchully-aboo!" The slogan of the O'Hanlons, hereditary standard bearers of Ulster. Derived from *Ard-choill*, high wood, or *ard-coille*, the height of the wood, probably some well-known hill that was the gathering place of the clan.

"Shanbodagh-aboo!" The old churl, was the battle cry of Magennis of Down.

No less famous in Irish annals than Clan Niall and Clan O'Donnell, were the Fitzgeralds, who, although of Norman blood, became "more Irish than the Irish themselves." The Geraldines were divided into two branches, of which the southern, or Desmond branch, had as their slogan "Shanid-aboo," from the massively constructed stronghold situated on the line of rounded hills running from north to south of County Limerick. From its commanding situation, by means of a signal fire lighted on the castle turret, intelligence or alarm could be conveyed over the whole of North Munster. The Earl of Desmond forfeited his princely patrimony in the sixteenth century, but the war cry has been retained by the knights of Glin, who use it as their motto.

The Leinster branch of the Geraldines had for their battle cry "Crom-aboo!"

Crom, the son of Maobrind, son of Ragnal [O'Donovan], built a castle on the river Maig, county Limerick, calling it by his own name. Subsequently, Maurice Fitzgerald, second Lord Offaly, overran that part of the country, and having taken the castle of Crom, adopted the war-cry or motto "Crom a buad" (not Crom-aboo), thus expressing his victory of Crom, the chief residence of a branch of the O'Donovans. He rebuilt the castle and made it his principal residence. When the head of the family became Earl of Kildare, he resided principally in the Pale, but the descendants of Maurice have retained the sound of the pronunciation in the incorrect spelling of "Crom-aboo!" as their battle-cry, and still their motto.

> "But not for rite nor feast ye stayed when friend or kin were pressed;
> And foemen fled when 'Crom Abu' bespoke your lance in rest."

Silken Thomas.

When in the year 1534 the Lord Deputy Garrett Oge Fitzgerald, Earl of Kildare, went into England in obedience to the king's mandate, he left his son, the young Lord Thomas, as Deputy in his place. On St. Barnabas' Day he rode through Dublin with one hundred and forty armed retainers, each wearing a silken fringe on his helmet, a mode of decoration which gave him the name by which he is best remembered. (Stanihurst.) This appointment of an inexperienced youth was a most unfortunate arrangement, as Kildare had left plenty of enemies behind him who now spread a report that he had been beheaded in England. This false report so incensed the young lord that entering the chamber where the Privy Council sat, he openly renounced his allegiance and proceeded to deliver up the sword and robes of state. His friend, Archbishop Cromer, now Lord Chancellor, with tears in his eyes besought him to forego his rash purpose. While this was taking place his Irish followers had thronged into the chamber, and becoming impatient of what was going on in a language that they did not understand, Neal Roe O'Kennedy, the Geraldine bard, was heard striking his harp, and chanting a lay in praise of "Thomas na Teeda" (the silken lord), and calling upon him to avenge his father's death:—

" 'Tis Thomas of the vest of silk, the raven of the vale,
The falcon of Kildare's tall towers, that scorns the mountain gale,
The raked up ember whose fierce flame shall prove the overthrow
Of every hungry Saxon dog—then "Farrah Crom-aboo!"

The bard's exhortation decided the fiery youth, and casting the sword of state upon the council table, he rushed forth with his men to engage upon that wild and hopeless struggle, which ended in the ruin of himself and his family.

The Fitzgeralds' great rivals and deadly enemies, the Butlers, Earls of Ormonde, had for their battle-cry, "Butler aboo!"

In the tenth year of Henry VII. there was passed "An Act abolishing these words, Cromabo and Butlerabo." This law remained in force until it was repealed by the Statues Law Revision (Ireland) Act, passed on August 13, 1878.

The Talbots of Malahide, cousins of "Silken Thomas," had for their motto and cry, "Prets d'accomplir."

In the rental book of Gerald, ninth Earl of Kildare, "The Lordship of Taghmooge, in Leix," we find "Baly Conlyn," whence perhaps, the O'More's slogan of "Conlan Aboo!"

This was O'More territory, but as the Geraldines waxed in greatness they claimed suzerainty over the O'Mores.

"The Fleming's Cry—Teine-ar-aghein-aboo. The business of fire to the bomb. *Aghein* properly signifies a kettle, but it is metaphorically used for a bomb or mortar.

. . . The words allude to their crest which is a Mortar piece casting out a Bomb with Flames of Fire, proper, Chains and Rings Or." (Ware: *Antiquities*, II., 163-4.)

"Poer aboo!" was the charging shout of the followers of Viscount Baltinglas, whose surname was Fitz-Eustace. The Fitzeustaces descended from the Anglo-Norman family of le Poer (now Power). A younger son of Sir Eustace le Poer, of Oughterard and Castlewarden, in county Kildare, assumed the Christian name of his father and called himself Fitzeustace, i.e., son of Eustace, but though the name was changed, the le Poer crest and war-cry (Poeragh aboo!) were still retained by the Eustace family.

The slogan of the De Burghs, or Bourkes of Connaught, was

"Gallruagh-aboo!" The red foreigner, taken, it is said, from "Iarla-Ruadh," Richard de Burgh, the red Earl of Ulster, who died in 1326. It is also sometimes given as "Gallriagh-aboo!" Riagh, a contraction of *riabhach*, swarthy, but the first seems the correct form.

"Gareach-aboo!" The war-cry of the Burkes of Clanwilliam. These Burkes lands in Munster included the most fertile portions of the present counties of Limerick and Tipperary, called after a progenitor of this powerful family, the Baronies of East and West Clanwilliam. He made his chief residence at Athassel, on the banks of the river Suir, in the midst of the Golden Vale of East Clanwilliam. Afterwards Castleconnell became their chief stronghold till the end of the eighteenth century.

The O'Carrols had "Slowac-aboo!" Slabhac (pro. *slowac*), a hawk. O'More's was "Conlan-aboo!" Conlan is mentioned in the Inquisitions as the name of a place in Queen's County. "Gear-laider-aboo!" Sharp and strong, was the cry of the Fitzpatricks, or M'Gilla Patricks, chieftains of Ossory.

"Faliagh-aboo!" was the slogan of O'Connor, while the Kavanaghs' shout was "Kinshelagh-aboo!" which referred to the men of Hy Kinshelagh, a clan inhabiting the mountainous and level country of which Mount Leinster was the centre, and deriving their name from Ceinseallach, their patriarch. They also had a second cry—"Clogheehy-aboo!"—"Dochy's stone." The chieftains of Hy Kinshelagh were inaugurated at Leagh M'Keogh, and this rock probably gave rise to their slogan.

"Geraldagh-aboo!" was the cry of Decies. Lord Decies was a Geraldagh, or Geraldine, as sprung from Gerald, eighth Earl of Desmond.

Tynsheog-aboo!" Tynsheog, the ash tree, used by the Delvin men. Delvin is the baronial title of Nugent, Marquis of Westmeath.

It is to be noticed that the war cries of the Barons of the Pale were in the Irish tongue, showing how, despite acts and ordinances, the English settlers were assimilated by the country. Thus the cry of County Louth settled by Norman chivalry on the borders of the Pale was "Shuyrym-aboo!" and the Shortalls "Puckan-sack-aboo!" Puckan signifies a sack or pouch, and the cry is perhaps an allusion to an armorial bearing. The Baron of Slane's cry was "Barncregan-aboo!" Perhaps a *bearna baoghail*, or pass of danger, well known as leading into Lord Fleming of Slane's country, and which this slogan called to defend.

"Fernock-aboo!" was the shout of the O'Toole's, from *fir*, or *fear-a-cnoic*, the men of the hill. An apt description for the brave clan Tuathail, who dwelt among the hills of northern Wicklow, it is recorded in "Grace's Annals" under A.D. 1316—"The Irish of Imayle (the glen of Imail in County Wicklow), attacked Tullow, and lost four hundred men, whose heads were brought to Dublin; marvellous things occurred, the dead rose again and fought with one another, shouting their cry after their fashion, "Fennok-aboo." Pembridge, "Annals Hiberniae;," has the same incident, and writes the word "Fennok-abo."

"Killole-aboo!" probably a *coille*, or wood, was used by the Doyles, or M'Dowells, of Arklow, who, like a great many of the sea-coast inhabitants, were of Danish extraction.

"Farliagh-aboo!" was the battle cry of the O'Connors of Offaley, and was derived from their remote ancestor, Failghe.

"Hussey, titular Baron of Galtrim,—Cor-deragh-aboe, perhaps the cause of the great Cast, alluding it may be to an Action of one of that family in the reign of Edward II., who at the battle of Athenry engaged and slew O'Kelly and his squire single-handed." (Ware: *Antiquities*, II., 163-4.)

In the County Tipperary the Anglo Irish family of the Purcells had for their slogan, "Pobal-puirsealach," *anglice* Pobble Purcell. This territory forms part of the territory of the barony of Eliogarty. The ruins of Purcell's magnificent mansion are to be seen close to the village of Loughma.

An interesting notice of the use of this war-cry is to be found in the State Papers, where there is an account of a clash that Purcell had with the authorities:—"Purcell, retiring backward from the sheriff, fell upon his back, and withal the sheriff fell upon him, and both being down and struggling together, Purcell lying undermost upon the ground, cried out to his men, 'Purcello Abo' (which is an invitation or call which the Irish lords use to their followers when they would have them to stick to them in any danger or distress). Thereupon divers of Purcell's men drew their swords and gave the sheriff sundry wounds in his head, whereof he died twenty-four hours after, and hurt divers of the sheriff's men." (*Cal. S.P.I.* pp. 114-15.)

The war-cry of the Heffernans was "Ceart na suas aboo!"

"Grassagh aboo!" was the slogan of the Graces of Courtstown, county Kilkenny.

> "O Courtstown! thy chieftains in kindness delight,
> As dauntless their valour, their glory is bright,
> In prowess unequalled they rush on the foe,
> While the hills and the vales ring with 'Grassagh Aboe!' "

"Roisteach-aboo!" The Roche's house or residence.

The Barrys appear to have used two war-cries—"Boutes en evant!" [Boutez-en-Avant] i.e., "Push forward," used by David de Barry to animate his men in a contest with the MacCarthys. This is said to be the derivation of the name of the town of Buttevant. The second—"Barragh aboo!" a man of the Barrys, is the one given in Dr. Meredith Hanmer's list of war-cries.

"Lamh-laidir aboo!" The strong hand aboo. The war-cry of the O'Briens, of Thomond. It was also used by the Fitzmaurice and M'Carthy clans, and must have caused extraordinary confusion whenever these three great southern clans met in conflict.

"Lasair Romhainn a Buadh!" The O'Mahony slogan.

A.D. 1088. Clan O'Mahony defeated a formidable combination of Norsemen organised to plunder Cork. . . The victory was a crushing one and verified the ancient battle-cry of the sept.

"Fustine-stelly-aboo!" was the battle-cry of the clan O'Suillivan, and that of the Knight of Kerry's men "Farre-buoy-aboo!" The yellow men, alluding perhaps to their saffron dyed linen shirts. At the present time the motto of the Knight of Kerry (Sir Maurice Fitzgerald) is "Mullacher-a-Buadh!"

"Fag-an-Bealach," vulgarly spelled "Faugh-a-Ballagh"—clear the way—was the cry with which the clans of Connaught and Munster used in faction fights to come through a fair with high hearts and smashing shillelaghs. The regiments raised in the South and West took their old shout with them to the Continental wars. It was the use of this *cri de guerre* by the old 87th (the Prince of Wales Irish) Regiment of Foot at the battle of Barossa, that caused the regiment, now the 1st Battalion Princess Victoria's (Royal Irish Fusiliers) to be nicknamed "The Old Fogs," or the "Faugh-a-Ballagh Boys." They also got the name of "The Eagle takers," or more shortly "Aiglers," from their capturing the eagle of the 8th French Light Infantry at Barossa. The regimental gazette is named "Faugh-a-Ballagh."

Modern progress in the art of fighting, as in other forms of human activity, has rendered the ancient war-crys, whether of Celtic chief or Norman knight, things of the past, subjects for the historian and the antiquary, and we could not if we would:—

"Bring back to life again, those hero-hosts so gay,
    Who fought with Conn the Hundred Fights—with Eo'gan urged the fray."

CHAPTER XXIX.

Names for the northern and southern halves of Ireland; characteristics of the four provinces.

Early in the second century the renowned Conn Ced Cathach (Kead Caha), or Conn of the Hundred Battles, became Ard Righ, or High King of Ireland, but notwithstanding his many fights he was not always successful, his most formidable antagonist being Eoghan Mor (Owen More). The latter is known by three other names, but only one of these concerns the present narrative—Mogh Nuadhat (pro. *Mow-Nooat*), King of Munster, who defeated Conn in ten battles and compelled him to divide the kingdom between them. For a boundary they fixed upon a continuous line of low hills running across the country from Dublin to Clarinbridge, in the county Galway, the northern half of which was ruled over by Conn, from which it was named Leth Chuinn, or "Conn's half," and the southern portion, Leth Mogha, that is "Mogh's half." The northern and southern portions of Ireland have in later days been characterised as "the Black North" and the "Sunny South."

Ireland, having got its two halves named, we may now proceed to deal with the four provinces. These are described in a rhyme as:—

> "Munster for the learning,
> Leinster for the beef,
> Connaught for a beggarman,
> And Ulster for a thief."

A variant of it is:—

> "The Leinster man is sprightly,
> The Munster man is boastful,
> The Connaught man sweet tongued,
> And the Ulster man impudent."

A third form is: —

> "Munster for learning, Connaught for breeding,
>   Ulster for thieving, and Leinster for feeding."

This rhyme does not seem to be very old, as in early times from the middle of the sixth till the ninth century, the period during which the great Irish schools were at the height of their fame, Munster had no preponderating number, and it is not till the eighteenth and from that till the early part of the nineteenth century that Munster became of special repute amongst the peasantry as a place of learning. T. Crofton Croker in "Researches in the South of Ireland," published in 1823, says:—"Amongst the peasantry classical learning is not uncommon, and a tattered Ovid or Virgil may be found in the hands of common labourers. In Munster the village schoolmaster forms a peculiar character; and next the lord of the manor, the parson, and the priest, he is the most important person in the parish. . . . With the schoolmaster, too, it is a matter of special pride to be visited by scholars from remote distances; it is not unusual to hear the respectability of a school estimated by the number of its stranger pupils." A very vivid and graphic description of that province "where the swallows fly in conic sections, and the magpies and turkeys confab in Latin, and the cows and bullocks will roar you Doric Greek," is given by William Carleton, in the story entitled "The Poor Scholar," ("Traits & Stories of the Irish Peasantry,") in which he depicts the experiences of a poor boy from the north of Ireland travelling to Munster in search of education. Leinster is famed for its rich grazing lands, while Connaught, with the exception of the county of Roscommon, is a much less fertile province. The allusion to "Ulster for a thief" is much less easy to explain, and cannot be elucidated by the writer. In ancient times Uladh, or Ulster, was designated by the literati as "the art loving province," as well they might, for by their arrogance and exorbitant demands they had provoked the people so far that the Ard Righ (High King) proposed that the Bardic order should be suppressed and its professors banished. This design to expel the poets was prevented by the seasonable intercession of Maolchabha, King of Ulster, who received them into his favour and saved them from banishment. This deliverance of the poets is recorded in the following lines:—

> "The valiant Maolchabha, King of Ulster,
> From exile sav'd by his authority,
> The poets of the island; in his province
> He entertained them, abandoned and forlorn,
> As the great patron of the Irish muse."

At the convention of Drumceat, held in 574, through the intercession of St. Columbcille, himself an Ulsterman, a compromise was effected, by which they were not banished, but their numbers were greatly reduced, and strict rules were laid down for their conduct in future.

The following poem, summing up the characteristics of the four provinces, appeared in "Walker's Hibernian Magazine," 1806, page 237:—

Connaught.

> "The Connaught man will get all he can,
> His impudence never has mist all;
>> Will seldomer flatter—
>> Than bully and batter;
> And he talks of his kin and his pistol.

Munster.

> A Munster man—is civil by plan,
> Again and again he'll entreat you;
>> Tho' you ten times refuse,
>> He his object pursues;
> Which is nine out of ten times to cheat you.

Ulster.

> An Ulster man—ever means to trepan,
> He watches your eye and opinion;
>> He will ne'er disagree,
>> Till his int'rest it be;
> And impudence marks his dominion.

Leinster.

A Leinster man—is all cup and can;
He calls t'other provinces knaves,
　　But each one of them see,
　　When he starts with the three,
His distance he frequently saves."

An expression common all over the north of Ireland is "Blackmouth," or "Blackmouthed Presbyterians." The origin of this epithet has never been cleared up. Some explain that in times of religious persecution in Scotland the Presbyterians were in many instances obliged for their safety to take to the hills, and that their mouths became stained or blackened by the wild fruits, such as blackberries, and blaeberries (whortleberries) on which they were obliged to subsist. "Blackmouth" must have been a well-known expression by the middle of the seventeenth century. In Wariston's *Diary* (Scottish Historical Society) edited by Dr. Hay Fleming, under date of 4th August, 1650, there is the following:—

"I blessed God that had given us a new Sabbath beyond and contrary to Cromwell's allowance, whose army sayd the last Sabbath that they would that day stoppe the blackmouth's (meaning God's servants) from rayling."

If the expression originated in Scotland, as it is not unlikely that it did, it is now practically obsolete in that country and confined principally to the north of Ireland. If it were used originally as a term of contempt or reproach, time has taken away its sting, and it is nowadays used in a half jocular fashion at which no offence is taken. William Carleton, who has stereotyped for all time the dialect of his native Tyrone as spoken in the early part of the nineteenth century, uses it in his sketch of "The Poor Scholar," referred to in a previous paragraph, as follows:—"We can aisaly put it off on some of these black-mouthed Presbyterians or Orangemen." W. B. Yeates in "Folk Tales," 1888, p. 187, has:—"The first marriage that happened between a blackmouth an' a catholic."

The larger dictionaries both of standard English, and of dialect, fail to throw any light on the origin of the term, but give "black-neb" which has a restricted currency in Scottish literature. There is in Scott's "Antiquary," 1816, p. 128:—"We shall set you down among the blac-nebs by and by." 'No, Sir Arthur, a tame grumbler.'"

The Wild Geese." This was the term applied to the Irish youth who enlisted in the Irish brigade under Louis XIV. of France, and his successors. The Catholic gentry cut off by the penal statutes from all hope of rising to distinction at home, sought promotion in foreign service, and those who thus left their native shores were termed "Wild Geese."

> "Oh! are they foam flakes on the ocean,
>   In the winds of early spring.
> Or are they trembling sails in motion,
>   Or wild geese on the wing?
>
> Oh! they're the wild geese, pretty daughter,
>   That fly before the spring—
> The wild geese o'er the roaring water—
>   The wild geese on the wing."

No doubt when the "Wild Geese," after campaigning "on far foreign fields from Dunkirk to Belgrade," returned on a visit to their native land, covered with wounds and glory, they were received by their relations with a "**Cead Mile Failte**." We have no knowledge of how old this characteristic welcome of the warm-hearted and hospitable Gael may be, but in the ancient form of "Eivlin a ruin" (Eveleen Aroon), by Carroll O'Daly, a bard who flourished in the fourteenth century, the last verse runs:—

> "Cead mile failte, here!
>   Eivlin a ruin!
> Cead mile failte, here!
>   Eivlin a ruin!
> A hundred thousand welcomes, dear,
> Nine hundred thousand welcomes here,
> O welcomes for ever here!
>   Eivlin a ruin!"   (Translation by Dr. Sigerson.)

In the reign of Queen Elizabeth the Irish question occupied the attention of the Government just as much as it did in the beginning of the twentieth century, and there was much resort at court of those employed in the government of Ireland, as well as of Irish chiefs and nobles, consequently in the works of Shakespeare, reflecting as they did the manners of the time, we find many references to Ireland and the Irish. In the tragedy of "Coriolanus," II., 1, 200, he uses the literal translation of the Irish greeting—"Ye're welcome all. A hundred thousand welcomes."

CHAPTER XXX.

Names under which Ireland was personified in the seventeenth century; the Emerald Isle.

The names enumerated sufficed the bards and senachies[24] in their allusions to Ireland so long as Irish literature and letters were centred in their own country and fostered by Irish chiefs and princes, afterwards native writers and literary men had a different centre, and a different point of view. The "flight of the Earls" was the first blow. The historians and bards that formed a part of the retinue of every great chief were now orphaned and beggared, the lands allotted to them in support of their profession confiscated and planted by alien strangers. Under these circumstances Ireland is alluded to under quite a new set of names. This is illustrated by "Roisin Dubh"—little black rose, an allegorical ballad in which strong political feelings are personified under the form of an address from a lover to his fair one. It was composed to celebrate Hugh Roe O'Donnell, and by "Roisin Dubh" (Roseen Duff), supposed to be a beloved female, was meant Ireland.

> "Oh! my sweet little rose, cease to pine for the past,
>   For the friends that come eastward shall see thee at last,
>   They bring blessings, they bring favours which the past never knew,
>   To pour forth in gladness on my Roisin Dhu."

The ruin of the Irish literary profession was practically completed by the rebellion of 1641, when such of the Gaelic chieftains and lords as had survived the Plantation period, were mostly ruined and driven into exile, and the driving out of the last Stuart king by William of Orange was the final blow. Under the penal laws naught was left to the Irish bard but his imagination, where he could take refuge in a more ethereal world from the hard realities of one in which he at present existed. It was this that buoyed him up, and in the depressing circumstances in which he found himself, caused him to sing of exalted greatness.

In these songs Ireland is alluded to as a beloved female of superlative beauty and charm, whose name must not be mentioned, and whose sorrows will yet end in most glorious triumph:—

> "Her sorrows fleeted—she struck the golden
> High-ringing harp with her snowy hand,
> And poured in music, the regal, olden,
> The lofty lays of a free-made land;
> The birds, the brooks, and the breeze seemed springing
> From grief to gladness that sunny dawn,
> And all the woods with delight were ringing,
> So sweet her singing for Bauhil Bawn!"

"The Blackbird" was well understood to mean Prince Charles Edward ("Bonnie Prince Charlie"), and was a poetic pretence common to both Scotland and Ireland.

> "Once on a morning of sweet recreation,
> I heard a fair lady a-making her moan,
> With sighing and sobbing, and sad lamentation,
> Aye singing, 'My Blackbird for ever is flown.'"

In these poems the Stuart Prince was a subsidiary personage, the agent for Erinn's deliverance, as in "Shiela gal (bright) ni Connolan."

> "Brave men and chiefs to lead them,
> Shall flash their spears in valour's van,
> And glorious days of freedom
> Crown Shiela gal ni Connolan."

Another name under which Ireland was personified by the Jacobite bards was "Kathleen Ni Houlahan."

> "Think her not a ghastly hag, too hideous to be seen,
> Call her not unseemly names, our matchless Kathaleen;
> Young she is and fair she is, and would be crowned a queen,
> Were the King's son at home here with Kathaleen Ni
> Houlahan."

Yet another name by which the poets voiced their hopes for Ireland was "Drimin."

> "Oh say, my brown Drimin, thou silk of the kine,
> Where, where are thy strong ones, last hope of thy line?
> Too deep and too long is the slumber they take,
> At the loud call of freedom, why don't they awake?"

(Translation by J. J. Callanan.)

Drimin is the favourite name of a cow, by which Ireland is here allegorically denoted. "Silk of the kine" is an idiomatic expression for the most beautiful of cattle, which has been preserved in the translation. This epithet reminds us that it was the impassioned lay of his bard, which in the sixteenth century decided the revolt of "Silken Thomas," or literally "Thomas of the silken vest," King Henry VIII.'s Lord Deputy in Ireland.

"Graunia Wael" is one of the endearing names given to Ireland during the Penal times. Named after Grace O'Malley, a famous heroine in Irish history and tradition, who flourished during the reign of Queen Elizabeth, to whom she paid a visit.

> "Above the bay, at dawn of day, I dreamt there came
> The beautiful—the wonderful—the dear bright dame!
> Her clustered hair, with lustre fair, lit all the vale—
> She came a star, with fame afar,
> Our Grainne Mael!"†
> *Sean Clarach MacDonnell.*
> Translation by Dr. Signerson [Sigerson].

"Maggie Laider." "This is another early sixteenth century name for Ireland, and signifies strong, or powerful Maggie. By an easy change the adjective, *laider*, strong, was converted into Lauder, the patrynomic of a Scottish family, and the air was employed to celebrate a famous courtesan of Crail." (Hardiman: *Irish Minstrelsy*, I., 177.)

---

† Pronounced as above (i.e. *Graunia Wael*), the "m" being modified.

The latter part of the eighteenth century, which saw the rise and decline of the Volunteers, followed by the rise of the United Irishmen, added little, with one notable exception, to the very considerable stock of names that Ireland had already accumulated. "The Shan Van Vogh," properly *An t sean bhean bochd*, meaning "poor old woman," seems to be about the only one.

> "Oh! the French are on the sea,
>   Says the Shan Van Vogh;
> The French are on the sea,
>   Says the Shan Van Vogh;
> Oh! the French are in the Bay, (Bantry)
> They'll be here without delay,
> And the Orange will decay,
>   Says the Shan Van Vogh."

There was an abortive French expedition towards the close of the year 1796, which would fix the date of the ballad.

Amongst a collection of street ballads purchased by T. Crofton Croker in Limerick, in 1821, there was one in which Ireland was allegorically styled "Cathaleen Thrail"—"Catherine the Slave."

Lastly we come to the poetical term for Ireland in most common use to-day:—

"The Emerald Isle."

Before A.D. 1185, an Irish author in Germany, of the life of Marianus Scotus, of Ratisbon, harks back to the "emerald isle," "the sweet soil of the native land"— dulce solum natalis patriæ . . . et verides terras (*Vita Mariani Ratisponensis*, I. (6; Boll. Feb. II. 366.).

In a Gaelic poem quoted by Douglas Hyde, in his "Literary History of Ireland," the appellation is partly anticipated in the following lines by an unknown sixteenth century poet:—

> "For born upon you, ye hosts of the Gael,
>   For your own Innisfail has been taken,
> And the Gall is dividing the 'emerald lands'
>   By your treacherous bands forsaken.

The foregoing is quoted as a mere coincidence, and has absolutely nothing to do with what Thomas Moore called "that rebellious but beautiful song, 'When Erin first rose.' " It is by Dr. William Drennan, a Belfast man, in whose poem entitled "Erin," written in 1795, the lines occur:—

> "Arm of Erin! prove strong; but be gentle as brave;
>   And uplifted to strike, still be ready to save;
>   Nor one feeling of vengeance presume to defile
>   The cause or the men of the **Emerald Isle**."

In a little volume entitled "Fugitive Pieces in Prose and Verse," by William Drennan, M.D., published in Belfast, March, 1815, the author in a note to the poem says he used the term "Emerald Isle" in a party song, written without rancour of party in the year 1795. From the frequent use made of the term since that time he fondly hopes that it will generally become associated with the name of his country as descriptive of its natural beauty and its inestimable value.

The patriotic author's aspiration has been gratified, and throughout the world, wherever the English language is spoken, by the name **Emerald Isle** Ireland is at once recognised as the country referred to. As is most fitting, the poet's association with the name of his country is happily referred to in the lines inscribed upon his tomb:—

> "Pure, just, benign, thus filial love would trace,
>   The virtues hallowing this narrow space—
>   The Emerald Isle may grant a wider claim,
>   And link the patriot with his country's name."

CHAPTER XXXI.

Earliest names of Ireland; Milesian names for the island; the Isle of Saints.

There can be very few countries or kingdoms that have, in addition to their usual name, so many poetical and descriptive designations as the kingdom of Ireland. The successive waves of colonisation, together with a quick-witted and imaginative people, have each contributed to this end. At the beginning of his history, Keating enumerates fourteen names for the country, the first being "Island of the Woods," or "Wooded Island," a name admirably descriptive of the forest-clad country down till the end of the reign of Elizabeth. The third name is **Inis Ealga**, that is, "noble island," which it is said to have borne during the Firbolg occupation. The Firbolgs were overcome by the Dedannans, who in their turn succumbed to the Milesians.

When the Milesians succeeded in landing upon the island in spite of the magic arts of the Tuatha de Dannans, the country was ruled over by three Dedannan princes, who reigned each for one year in their turn. The names of their wives were Banbha, Fodhla, and Eire. After landing, the invading force marched to a mountain called Sliabh Mis; here they were met by Banbha, attended by a train of beautiful ladies, and followed by her druids and sooth-sayers. Amirgin, the Milesian, addressed himself to her and desired to have the honour of knowing her name. She answered her name was Banbha, and from her the island was called Inis Banbha. (It was also sometimes styled by the bards, Ard-Banbha—high Banbha.)

From thence they proceeded on their march and arrived at Sliabh Eibhlin, where the princess Fodhla met them with a retinue of ladies and druids about her; they desired to know her name, and she replied that her name was Fodhla, which was also the name of the island. It was from this princess that Ollamh Fodhla (Ollav Fola), who was one of the wisest and greatest of the pagan kings of Ireland, was named. He had been first a learned Ollamh, or Doctor,‡ and afterwards king of Fodhla, or Ireland.

They went on and came to Usnach, where they were met by Eire and her attendants. She was likewise desired to discover her name, and she told them her name was Eire, and from her the country was called Eire. It is said that these three queens were sisters, and married to three brothers, amongst whom there was an agreement that each brother should alternately take his year of government, and during the year of his reign the isle should be called after the name of his queen. The reason that it is called Eire more frequently than Banbha or Fodhla being that the husband of Queen Eire, from whom the island was called Ireland, happened to be king at the time it was conquered by the sons of Milesius. From Eire is derived Erin, the dative case of the name, and Ireland.

The Clanna Mileadh, or children of Milesius, having conquered Ireland, renamed the island "Scotia," after their mother, Scota, the widow of King Milesius, who accompanied her sons and who was slain three days after their landing in Ireland, in a battle at Sliabh Mis, in which the Milesians, under the command of Heber, one of the sons of Miledh, were attacked by a strong body of Tuatha de Dannans, commanded by Queen Eire, whom, after a severe fight, they defeated. There was great loss on both sides, Queen Scota being the most notable on that of the Milesians, of whom an ancient bard has written:—

> "Mixed with the first the fair Virago fought,
>   Sustained the toils of arms and danger sought."

From her son, Eibhear Fionn (the fair), or Heber, who commanded in this battle, the name "Hibernia" is said to be derived.

In a subsequent battle the combined forces of the Tuatha de Dannans, under their three kings and queens were utterly routed, the three kings slain, also their consorts, who had given their names to Ireland.

---

‡ There were doctors of the several professions; just as we have Doctors of Law, Medicine, Literature, etc. The full course of study for an ollave was twelve years.

It was the usual custom for kings and queens in those days to not only command in battle, but fight side by side with their forces, male and female, for the clanswomen fought as well as the men, and were only exempted from military service in the year 590, through the influence of Columbcille, at the Synod of Druimceat. Notable instances are, in Irish history, Queen Macha, of the golden hair, who founded Armagh; and in British history, Queen Boadicea, whose heroic resistance to the Romans has immortalised her name.

The bardic derivation of "Scotia," from Scota, daughter of Pharoh, and wife of Milesius, manifestly betrays its Christian origin.

The name "Scotia" belonged exclusively to Ireland till the tenth century, prior to which the Irish colonised Argyllshire. These colonists being harassed and oppressed, by the Picts, called to their assistance Niall of the Nine Hostages, who came with a numerous army to their aid. When he arrived he changed the old name of the country (Albu or Alban) and called it "Scotia," at the request of the Dalriads and Scots themselves; but it was agreed that it was to be called "Scotia Minor," while "Scotia Major" was to be the name of Ireland. When Fergus, commonly called Fergus MacErc, became king of the Scottish Gallic colony, which ultimately mastered the whole country, the name Scotia was applied to it instead of being confined, as formerly, to the portion colonised by the Gaels from Scotia Major, or Ireland. The transference of the name "Scotia" from Ireland to Scotland seems to have been an accomplished fact prior to the eleventh century, for Mariannus Scotus, who lived from 1028 to 1081, calls Malcolm II., who died 1034, "rex Scotae" (*Chron. Picts and Scots*, p. 65), and Brian, King of Ireland, "rex Hiberniae."

Ireland was also known as "the plain of Ir," from Ir, another of the sons of Miledh, who was one of the commanders of the Milesians in their invasion of Ireland. When the invading fleet approached the shores of the island, the Tuatha de Dananus, by means of their magical arts raised a violent tempest in which the ship commanded by Ir was separated from the rest of the fleet and driven upon the western coast of Munster, where it split upon the rocks and every man on board perished. From Ir descended the noble clan Rury, whose magnificent court was held at Emain Macha (Armagh), and from whom sprang the Red Branch Knights, famous in song and story.

"**Inis Fail**," the isle of destiny, another name for Ireland, so called from the stone, *Lia Fail*, on which the Irish monarchs were crowned prior to its removal to Scotland for the crowning of Fergus MacErc. It is generally accounted to be this stone that now forms the seat of the coronation chair in Westminster Abbey.

> "Unless the fix'd decrees of fate give way,
>   The Scots shall govern and the sceptre sway,
>   Where'er this stone they find and its dread sound obey."

"**Isle of Saints**." For three centuries, from the fifth to the ninth, the civilisation of Europe belonged to Ireland, says a German historian. During this period Erinn became an island of learning, studded with great schools, while Irish missionaries were to be found all over Europe.

NOTES

Chapter I

[1] *beetle*: a type of wooden mallet.

[2] *pratie*: a potato.

[3] *bap*: a roll of bread.

[4] *black lumps*: in another (probably later) version of the rhyme 'black balls' (clove balls) is used.

Chapter VII

[5] *bawbees*: halfpennies in the old coinage.

Chapter X

[6] *capons*: castrated male chickens.

[7] *deil*: devil.

Chapter XII

[8] *Tyrone among the bushes*: The author Lydia Mary Foster used this line for the title of one of her books, published in 1933.

Chapter XIII

[9] *gabbocks*: a type of fish. According to the *Dictionary of the Scots Language*, as reported in the *Dumfries Weekly Journal*, December 22nd, 1789, they are 'about half a yard long, and very fat to eat, and have no fins on them'.

———◆———

[10] This rhyme is quoted in an introductory essay to *Robert Huddelston, Bard of Moneyrea: Selected Songs and Poems* (Belfast: Ullans Press, 2014), p. xxii, but with a variant third line—'and twenty shillin's to the pound'.

[11] *Sneddin' turnips*: i.e., cutting off the tops and roots.

[12] *Morgan Rattler*: Sir John Byers refers to this term on p. 6 of his *Sayings, Proverbs and Humour of Ulster*. Among the Robert Huddleston (1814-1887) collection at the Ulster Folk and Transport Museum is an (as yet) unpublished poem called 'McMullan's adieu to his auld horse Morgan Rattler' which confirms that the epithet was applied to horses.

Chapter XVI

[13] *Gin*: an old Scots form of 'if'.

Chapter XIX

[14] The title of the book is actually *The Wonderful Prophecies of Robert Nixon, the celebrated Cheshire Prophet.*

Chapter XXIII

[15] *Soop*: Scots for 'sweep'.

[16] *shool*: a variant of the Scots *schule* meaning 'to shovel'.

[17] *middin'*: i.e. 'midden', a dunghill or compost heap.

[18] *whin*: a prickly gorse with yellow flowers.

Chapter XXIV

[19] This is a reference to *The General History of Ireland* by Jeoffrey

Keating, translated (from the Irish) by Dermod O'Connor (London/Dublin, 1723).

[20] Turlough O'Carolan (1670-1738), the blind Irish harper.

Chapter XXV

[21] *foother*: a bungler or clumsy person; as a verb it means to fiddle about, potter around.

Chapter XXVI

[22] *laverock*: skylark.

[23] *gowk*: another name for the cuckoo, but can also mean a fool or simpleton.

Chapter XXX

[24] *senachies*: story-tellers.

Printed in Great Britain
by Amazon.co.uk, Ltd.,
Marston Gate.